Abracadabra

The Steve Miller Story

Marc Shapiro

Abracadabra

The Steve Miller Story

Marc Shapiro

WYMER
PUBLISHING
Bedford, England

First published in Great Britain in 2024
by Wymer Publishing
www.wymerpublishing.co.uk
Tel: 01234 326691
Wymer Publishing is a trading name of Wymer (UK) Ltd

Copyright © 2024 Wymer Publishing.

ISBN: 978-1-915246-48-6
(also available in eBook)

Edited by Jerry Bloom

The Author hereby asserts his rights to be identified
as the author of this work in accordance with sections
77 to 78 of the Copyright, Designs & Patents Act 1988.

All rights reserved. No part of this publication may be
reproduced or transmitted in any form or by any means,
electronic or mechanical, including photocopying, or any
information storage and retrieval system, without written
permission from the publisher.

This publication is sold subject to the condition that it shall not,
by way of trade or otherwise, be lent, re-sold, hired out or
otherwise circulated without the publishers prior consent in any
form of binding or cover other than that in which it is published
and without a similar condition including this condition
being imposed on the subsequent purchaser.

Every effort has been made to trace the copyright holders of the
photographs in this book but some were unreachable. We would
be grateful if the photographers concerned would contact us.

Typeset by Andy Bishop / Tusseheia Creative.
Printed by CMP, Dorset, England.

A catalogue record for this book is available from the British Library.

Cover design: Tusseheia Creative
Front cover photo © Gijsbert Hanekroot / Alamy Stock Photo

Contents

Author's Notes: An Argument Could Be Made	9
Introduction: No Samples, No Loops, None Of That Shit	13
The Jazz-happy Parents	17
Learning The Ropes	21
Les And Steve: The Whole Damned Story	25
Dallas Shock Treatment	29
T-Bone On The Menu	31
Age Five: A Musician Until He Dies	33
St. Marks, Get Set, Go	35
The Marksmen Open Fire	39
Evolution On The March	43
Miller's Out Of Here	47
Steve Miller Is In All The Bands	49
Name: Steve Miller. Occupation: Radical.	53
Steve Hits Chicago... Chicago Hits Back	55
Hanging With The Fishes	59
Miller, Goldberg, Hullabullo, Goodbye	61
You Need To Come Here Now	65
Monterey Pop: The Miller Report	67
He Loves Chuck... He Loves Chuck Not	69
What They Were Expecting Were Dummies	71
Wild In The UK	75
Sailor Makes Hits, Loses Friends	81
In A Hurry For A Brave New World	87
An Offer Too Good To Refuse	89
Brave New World And On And On	93
Call An Ambulance	101
The Joker's On You	105
Choices To Make	109
Fly Like An Eagle	111
If You Blinked You Missed This	115

Take The Money And Run	117
Rockin' Me Don't Bother Me	121
Book Of Dreams... That's Odd	123
It's My Song... You Do It	125
Jungle Love... Share And Share Alike	127
Swingtown... The Last Roundup	129
Dazed Days	131
Floundering In A Circle Of Love	133
Abracadabra... The End Of An Era	137
Can You Top This?	141
All Work And All Play	147
Miller Goes It Alone	151
Hit The Road, Steve	155
Miller's Way Or The Highway	157
Miller Gives McCartney A Hand	159
Attitude Adjustment: 1993-2010	161
Bingo! Let Your Hair Down	165
Divorce/Marriage: Steve Miller Style	167
An Apple For Professor Miller	169
The Landed Gentleman	171
Miller Makes Peace... Sort Of	173
The Hits Are Back	175
A Deep Dive Into The Vault	177
Them's Fighting Words	179
Slipping Into The Future	183
The End: It's That Simple	185
Appendix	187
They're In The Band	190
Discography	190
Sources	191

Author's Notes:
An Argument Could Be Made

Being first is an instant turn-on.
First in life. First in love. First at the track, especially when that fifty-to-one longshot comes in, well, first. First is something special. You've done it when nobody else has. First is something that can't be beat. First puts you in the record books. First is forever.

And most especially in the world of the celebrity biography author. Being first, in the ever-expanding universe of instant this and instant that, it does on occasion happen that a true first in the world of celebrity authorship does happen. And on occasion it has happened to me.

When the Canadian rock band The Tragically Hip suddenly, after years of regional obscurity, emerged as critically and marginally hip, I smashed and dashed out a biography of the band that was truly, despite a Canadian publisher's insistence that they were the first, was out the door first.

On the darker side, when Latina singer Jenni Rivera's plane went down, another first came with a phone call six hours after the crash, requesting a Jenni Rivera book in six weeks. I won't lie to you and say that I felt a little bit of a ghoul at the prospect. But I had some mouths to feed so I jumped on the gig and six weeks to the day, my Jenni Rivera book was, indeed, the first of several that would follow in short order to good reviews and sales.

Which brings us to right now and the offer to be the first kid on the literary block to chronicle the life and times of rocker Steve Miller with Abracadabra: The Steve Miller Story. The good folks at Wymer Publishing sweetened the offer with the insistence that this would be the absolute first Steve Miller biography on the planet and who was I to doubt that?

Well, I'll be honest with you: I doubted a little. First in anything is hip, gear and groovy. But first in reality is a whole other animal.

Steve Miller, in the eyes of many and countless, has been far from below the radar for decades and he's been far from bashful in strutting his stuff. He always tours. He always records. He's been good for a radio-friendly hit on a fairly consistent basis. Steve Miller has always been out and around in the public's consciousness. So surely some scribe must have long ago set this cat's story down. So, in a perfect world, why shouldn't it be me?

In a sense, there had long been the possibility that the first ever biography on Steve Miller might well have been an autobiography by Miller himself at a time when, truth be known, there was not a whole lot to write about. As Miller once conceded in conversation with Pollstar.Com, "It's the book that everybody always thought I should do. I've been reading biographies for a long time and thinking about writing my own. When I was in college, learning about comparative literature and creative writing, I was going to be a writer, a teacher and a journalist. I went one semester of not having a band and I went 'nope. This is not going to work for me. I got to play music. Writing a book is a serious project. I'm serious about it and one day I'll do it'."

Sorry Steve. Beatcha' to it.

And before I set out to write one word, I did a bit of self-examination in an attempt to answer the question of just what it was that I liked about this guy. And the answer to the question was quite simple. He was real. Let's start with the music, a throwback in this day and age, Steve Miller has always been about visceral licks, clever and to-the-point lyrics and vocals that always seemed to make creative and commercial sense. There was a reason Miller was a natural attraction in Top Forty radio. It was relatable, hummable and eats up three minutes and under while driving down the highway at warp speed. In the best possible sense, Steve Miller was one of us.

Live was equally an acknowledgement to everything that performers had always been about. Years before pyro and the first hints of makeup and outlandish physical effects became de regur, Miller's schtick was time honoured and traditional, strutting the stage, the exaggerated gyrations, the facial grimaces going hand and hand with the music. Miller live was a very human and emotional marriage of the now and what it meant to connect with an audience riled up for a night of rock that drew them in and refused to let go.

Now I had the answer. I was a fan.

I set to work on the matter, exploring the Steve Miller bibliography until I had brain freeze.

I spent a good bit of time on the Internet and would come up with mixed results on the question of whether I would truly come first or trail a distant second. The fact was that there were several of those song books that showed aspiring musicians the chord changes and all the nuts and bolts of playing Miller's greatest hits (1973-76 when Miller's commercial/radio friendly prowess was in full flower and bookended by hits as early as 1968 and as late as 1982).

But while Miller liked to talk and there was plenty of insightful anecdotes to be found, at the end of the day there was no full-blown biography to be found. But now there is.

I took the gig, began the prerequisite boatload of research, tracked down people, primarily in old, published memories, who would talk the talk and spent many a sleepless nights humming along to the likes of 'Jungle Love', 'Living In The USA', 'Jet Airliner' and a whole lot of others. At points, there seemed to this author that Steve Miller was a prolific so and so who just could not help himself.

But I persisted. Busted my literary chops and emerged with the story some six months later. If there was even a hint of a stone left unturned, I can assure you that I found it. The big challenge was getting Miller to talk the talk for what would be a totally unauthorised biography. Would he talk the talk or would I walk the walk? You shall see.

Abracadabra: The Steve Miller Story delves deeply into the musicians' entire bit of business, much of which lies well below the surface of the obvious biographical tropes of sex, drugs and rock and roll. By turns, Miller is a quiet, to-the-point deep thinker. He comes from a period that has deep musical roots and he has cultivated them well.

Miller is very much a traditionalist, steeped in the blues, jazz and everything that came well before the coming of The Beatles, psychedelia and the summer of the sixties that predated modern rock. And it has been a period that the singer/guitarist has been adamant in hanging on to.

Even as the audiences have continued for decades to clamour for the hits, Miller has made it plain at every opportunity, including interviews at The New Orleans Jazz And Heritage Festival and Elsewhere.com, to extoll the virtue of traditional jazz, blues and the original long hair music. Rock and roll as a smart man's game that people who want to stay in the game well into their seventies rather than be one and done.

"I've been doing it (concerts) for fifty years," a very tongue-in-cheek Miller recalled in 2018. "There are fourteen songs I always need to play. I want my audiences to hear what they want to hear. The trick is to weave that other nine songs into the set. I want to keep them entertained and excited to see us the next time we come to town."

Marc Shapiro 2024

Abracadabra

Introduction:
No Samples, No Loops, None Of That Shit

Getting to the heart and soul of Steve Miller, how he acts emotionally, as a salient human being who interacts just about any old way that moves him, may seem on the surface to be a near impossible nut to crack.

In a philosophical and psychological sense, understanding Steve Miller – whether in the music scene, professionally, or during casual moments with family and friends, strumming old blues tunes and leaving them impressed by his easy-going nature – is akin to chasing Mercury on a breezy day. Steve Miller is both complex and unpredictable, yet at the same time, he's just an ordinary guy.

Who comes part and parcel with a defiant, combative, my-way-or-the-highway streak.

Every time you turn around, you find Steve Miller attitude for days. And it's not always attitude that is well measured or mannered. Miller is a cool cat, easy to get along with and amenable to a fair thee well. But, in the same creative breath, highly principled, a personality who doesn't think twice about mixing it up when something rubs him the wrong way.

Such was the case when Miller explained Miller explained to The Washington Post how he managed to get through it all with his teeth, money and principles intact. He was quick to acknowledge a number of examples of how he was rock and roll smart rather than rock and roll not so smart. "I've always been keen on what I can control. I have never played gigs at a discount and, as early as my teenage years, with a pickup high school band, I was making money doing it."

For such a young kid, Miller possessed an instinctive combination of talent and a bottom line sense of business and making things happen. Veteran rock historian Bruno Ceriotti, whose numerous detailed and insightful day-by-day diary formats have appeared in weebly.com, blogspot and pinterest.com was particularly effective in chronicling the early years of Steve Miller, which offered up an interview with Miller on how his business smarts came into play in those early gigs with his first real pro band The Marksmen.

"There weren't any rock and roll bands in those days. So, I sent out mimeographed letters out to sororities, fraternities, church schools and synagogues, any place where they had music. I said, 'I've got a rock and roll band and I'm looking to book them for the next three weeks and I ended up booking the band for half a year in just three weeks.'"

As he grew into his post high school years, there was seemingly more to Steve Miller than bravado and cocksuredness. His rapidly maturing musical acumen was matched only by a sense of self and just how the business side of pop music worked and, by association, how Miller played the game. By 1967, Miller found himself in the middle of a rock and roll signing frenzy in which anybody who could play three chords of a guitar, had long hair and had a Bay Area zip code was ripe for the picking as major record labels lined up to make their bid. Miller, in a talk around with the Steve Miller Band.com, admitted to a high degree of naivety as well as confidence in what he wanted.

That Steve was so business astute at such an early age had much to do with the fact that he always listened to his elders, which in his case, was a wide array of well-known musicians who had played the game and had won some and lost some. Greg Fischbach, Miller's attorney during the early seventies told The Washington Post as much when he offered, "Steve's impression of the music industry has always been right and that impression was that the business side basically took advantage of the artists."

Adding an equally succinct description of Steve Miller as all business all the time was musician Les Dudek, who appeared for a time with The Steve Miller Band in the seventies. He told The Washington Post "Steve paid for everything and he paid in cash. He had all kinds of trusts set up."

Consequently he was surprising to the label honchos, when he signed his first contract as he recalled in SteveMillerBand.com, "Admittedly I was still very naïve. I mean it was 1967 and I was still a kid and I had fourteen record companies trying to sign me, but I knew what I wanted. So I said I wanted to have total artistic control over everything I did, I wanted to own my own publishing and I wanted a half million dollars."

Once the labels picked their jaws up from the floor at the audacity of Miller's demands, Capitol Records blinked, and Miller got his deal. To say that Miller was a bit full of himself by the time he entered the Capitol Records recording studios for his band's very first recording session was an understatement as he surveyed the studio and the handful of preppie looking engineers that headed up the music department.

"There was an immediate attitude problem," Miller said in SteveMillerBand.Com. "They thought I was some kind of hippie and immediately walked out of the session. I went to my producer and told him that I would give up my upfront money in exchange for having total creative control of the album. And that included the session producer of my choice."

Corporate Capitol got the hint and Miller got engineer Glynn Johns and recording dates in Olympic Studios in England. Miller had read the contract, and he knew Capitol did not have a leg to stand on. It would be one of many battles that Miller would have with the fine print side of the music business, and he would come away from the experience with what he would consider rule number one in rock and roll, as he disclosed in Brainy Quotes.com, "Never sign a contract you can't get out of and never give your songs away."

Well into his eighties, Miller remains steadfast in his career-long crusade to doing right by his own attitudes and beliefs. In an American Songwriter interview, he would reflect on the fact that talent, self-belief and confidence in his ability bring him so much that continues to last. And that continues to surprise him.

"My whole career has been a surprise," he conceded as he contemplated entering his eighth decade. "I'm still playing for some reason and I still feel great."

And he offered in a collection of BrainyQuotes.Com that it all begins when he steps on the stage. "I play for the audience's pleasure. What I expect from them is not important. What they expect from me is important."

And what Steve Miller has given them is the real thing, as he explored in Pollstar.com, "We're not out to screw around. We're there to play a lot of live music for real. No samples. No loops. None of that kind of shit. Just perform and play real."

Abracadabra

The Jazz-happy Parents

It was the forties. Conflict was in the air and lurking around every corner. Emotions and opportunity were there for the taking. There was love and romance and the notion that opposites attracted. Prime examples were Steve Miller's parents, George and Bertha Miller.

Miller quickly picked up as he quoted in Weebly.com, BrainyQuotes.com, AcademicsOfDictionariesAndEncyclopedias.com and Guitar World, how he had been born into a household of music and musicians.

"We were a very different family," Miller chronicled in Offbeat Magazine. "I often wondered what made my parents different from other adults. My parents were raised in Missouri near a place called Jefferson City. They were like country people, but the difference was that they were also musicians. On my mother's side, everyone played piano and I had an uncle who played jazz violin in an orchestra. They were just dirt-poor farmers and I always wondered how these hillbillies from Missouri became so hip? How did they know all this music stuff? It was all about the radio. They were as hip as they could be about things like Kansas City Jazz and they had a record collection that wouldn't stop."

Miller would recall in Offbeat Magazine and Brainy Quotes.com that his father was a whirlwind when it came to finding any number of ways to make a living.

"My father was a pathologist who was also a hat salesman, a master electrician, a master mason, a master carpenter and a master boat builder. He was also a kind of music nut who had a phenomenal knowledge of music. Back in the day, he had a tape recorder, called a Magnacorder, which was like having something from Mars. My dad was kind of a hipster and a doctor. And he always had a great hi-fi system."

In the post World War II days, like most others who had settled in Milwaukee, the Miller family were industrious and self-sufficient and, by degrees, religious. Family gatherings were part and parcel of the Miller lifestyle, which, in one way or another, seemed to centre around music.

But it would be those early days that would reinforce the fact that Miller's earliest influences came from his mother's side of the family as he would reflect in Weebly.com and Country Line Magazine. "My mother was a very jazz influenced singer. I was born into a household where everybody lived their music. Besides singing, my mother played piano and sang harmony with her two sisters while her brothers played guitar, banjo and violin." (16)

In Elsewhere.co.nz Miller would point with pride to his musical roots. "I was really fortunate because my parents loved music. My mother's brother had the first real professional gig playing for the Paul Whiteman Orchestra and my dad just loved blues and jazz and my mom (as he reflected in an interview with television journalist Dan Rather} "had a great voice. She sounded a lot like Ella Fitzgerald."

The Miller family, musical passions aside, still had real world issues to deal with. Money was forever tight with George's medical job offering a comfortable lifestyle. However, never far from the surface of their day-to-day lives was all things musical, with George sticking to his goal of somehow, someway, aspiring to do something with music. "My father had a phenomenal knowledge of music, especially blues and jazz," he told radio personality Howard Stern, "Even though they didn't have a lot of money."

Slowly but surely, an idea began to take shape in the Miller household. George decided that he would use his newfound toy, the Magnacorder, to try his hand at being a recording engineer. Along with his easy-going attitude that made forming relationships with musicians fairly easy, he could use his knowledge of the technical aspects of recording live performing and studio musicians. The Millers now had a plan.

"My dad would just go out to the clubs and see people play and he would just ask the musicians if he could just bring his tape recorder along and they would always say 'yeah sure,'" recalled Miller in Offbeat. "There was never a problem about that."

George and Bertha had a surprise early in 1943 when Bertha announced that she was pregnant. The ensuing months would be a chaotic, joyous experience and, on 3rd October, Steven Miller came kicking and wailing into the world. He was on time and, by all accounts, his pitch was perfect. Miller, who never had to search far for the humour and irony in any situation would later acknowledge the historical perspective on his birth in an interview with SteveMillerBand.com. "I was born in 1943. They dropped the atomic bomb in 1945. That was the end of the war."

It would not be long after that Miller, in conversation with Pollstar.com, recalled the instinctive musical tie between child and

parents that almost immediately developed.
"I don't know how my parents got to be so hip. But they were."

Abracadabra

Learning The Ropes

One thing you could say about Steve Miller, is that there was no arguing with the fact that he was one hell of a bright and perceptive baby. He was barely out of nappies when he was soaking up every aspect of the Miller family's musical lifestyle.

He did not always understand what was going on: the family sing-a-longs, brothers, sisters and assorted relatives showing up and plucking various stringed instruments, and music of all kinds playing cool and blustery out of record players and radios. All he knew was that it played way positive in his head by newborn standards.

And when the Miller family noticed his interest, they were quick to invite Steve to join in.

"I was born into a household where there was music just about everywhere I turned," he reflected in BrainyQuotes.com. and The Dallas Observer. "It was like my aunt; my grandmother and my mother lived their music and they were always singing harmony while my mother would play the piano. By the time I was two, I was joining in and singing three-part harmony on the song 'Row Row Row Your Boat'. In a sense, you could say that I was born to be a musician. It seemed like I was surrounded by music all my life."

But while Bertha and the rest of the Miller musical clan were nurturing Steve's creative drive, it would be his father, George, who would offer up a more practical, but just as passionate, approach. George had set about making his drive to become a recording engineer a reality when, not long after buying the Magacorder, he would set up a workable professional recording studio in his house. Then came the aspect of his plan that George seemed to relish the most.

George and Bertha had long ago become regulars at the local jazz and blues clubs. His sincerity and personable nature inevitably won over any number of name headliners as they passed through the local club and concert scene. He would win them over with the promise of a home cooked meal, an occasional place to spend the night and the opportunity to have their live and/or studio performance recorded under professional conditions with first rate equipment by a technically knowledgeable fan who knew his stuff. Among those who would take George and the Miller clan up on their offer between

1945-1948 were such notables as Charles Mingus, Tal Farlow and Red Norvow.

At the ripe old age of four, Miller was not quite getting the emotional significance of all these strangers popping in and out of the house and playing music. But, in conversation with Let'sSingIt.com, he acknowledged a sense of importance in his psyche. "They would just come and hang out on a Sunday afternoon. I saw the respect my dad had for them and it seemed like musicians were just the greatest people of all."

At the age of five, Miller could only watch in wonder as the daily comings and goings in the Miller household were filled with music and the musicians of note who stopped by for impromptu sessions and recordings, conspicuous by the fact that the atmosphere offered by the Millers was conducive to some of the biggest names in jazz and blues acting like normal people who were just as capable of asking 'can you pass the peas and carrots' as they were playing an inspiring bit of musical business. Steve would be intent as he watched the dichotomy of stardom and humanity unfold. He was getting it.

1949 would be a pivotal year in popular music. The stalwarts, Spike Jones, Dinah Shore, Perry Como, Vic Damone and Frankie Laine among others, were continuing to hold sway on the pop charts and very much in an old school way. But it would become obvious that 1949 saw the rumblings of a new way of doing things. 'The Fat Man' by Fats Domino would be the first ever recording to contain a driving backbeat all the way through.

'When Things Go Wrong With You (It Hurts Me Too)' by Tampa Red was showing its deeper possibilities and no less a personage than Elmore James would be one of many who would tackle the raw blues attitude of the song.

What was going on musically was not lost on the impressionable young boy. The concept of music being something that was not only enjoyable in a family way was teasing at Miller's psyche as something that could be a person's work. Miller reflected on those feelings during an interview on the CBS Sunday Morning News, "I know at that point that I didn't want to be a rock star. I just wanted to be a musician."

1949 was the first sign that the torch was being passed. It was also the first time that Steve Miller picked up a guitar that was truly his own that figuratively, and finally literally, he would not let go. In a 2010 interview that was excerpted for Bruno Cerritos' massive look at Steve Miller's early years, Miller, with a small amount of drama and irony thrown in for good measure, told the tale.

"Dr. Dale Atterbury, an uncle who played in the well-known Paul

Whiteman Orchestra, came to the house for a few days for a visit and brought along this Gibson archtop guitar. It was a sweet little guitar. It was the first guitar I ever had my hands on. My uncle stayed for five days. When my uncle was getting ready to leave the night before, I was terrified that he wasn't going to leave the guitar. He would leave early the next morning. After he left, I went downstairs. There was the guitar case behind the couch. That sweet little honey-coloured guitar."

"He had left it for me."

Abracadabra

Les And Steve:
The Whole Damned Story

Groupie. The word was probably coined somewhere around 1965 by rock star Frank Zappa to describe women and young girls who pursued their favourite rock bands and musicians sexually and in other ways. However, a case could also easily be made that the definitive definition of Groupie went by a number of different derivations and that was around as far back as 1948, and that Steve Miller's father George was a prime example of the form.

To wit, George Miller was a fan. Whenever the big-time jazz musicians and blues bands of the day were on tour, George, and by degrees, Bertha could be counted on to be in the proverbial front row. But George would take it a bit further when the potential of his passion coupled with his newfound mania for technology and recording had seemingly pushed him into that grey area.

It would take a connection with up-and-coming duo Les Paul and Mary Ford for George's plan to truly spring into action. As chronicled by countless publications including the Milwaukee Journal Sentinel, Paul and his soon-to-be wife Ford were on hiatus from the never-ending Hollywood hustle and had taken up residency at a Milwaukee night club called Jimmy Fazio's Town Room, the better to brainstorm an act that would sit well with television executives in New York. Not surprisingly, it wasn't long before George got wind of the buzz around Paul and Ford and was soon a regular fixture at Jimmy Fazio's. It was not long before George approached the couple with his sincerity and a plan.

"My father loved music and he had this tape recorder," Miller recalled in the Milwaukee Journal Sentinel. "He offered to record some of their performances, and they said they'd like that." Those privy to the recording sessions echoed the notion that they could be professional and that the atmosphere during those sessions was very much a family affair in which Steve was allowed to be present in his father's makeshift studio whilst the completed recordings were played. And, as he remembered in the Milwaukee Journal Sentinel, it was, for the then four-year-old, heaven on earth.

"It was great to be a four-year-old sitting there watching Les and my dad do this thing. It was great at age four to watch them and realise how hip it was."

The Paul/Miller relationship evolved quite naturally into an almost communal atmosphere, regular visits and a whole lot of music time. Les and Steve, with music as a common denominator, became quite close. It seemed like the two were always joined at the hip, with Les showing Steve some of the basics of chording as they sat guitar to guitar, and Les taking on the role of musical Godfather in the young Miller's mind.

The daily shows at Jimmy Fazio's Town Room had also, quite naturally, evolved into a family affair with Steve, going on five, regularly in the club, sitting rapt and transfixed as Les Paul and Mary Ford did their thing, often to the accompaniment of other musicians. Miller would often recall those moments when he would sit on a stool close to the stage and watch the magic. He said in a 2018 interview, "I was growing up, seeing people playing music. So I thought that was the most radical thing in the world to do."

Miller would ultimately acknowledge in The Oklahoman, that those regular nights watching Les Paul and Mary Ford and a vast array of talented musicians who came in and out of the scene would be a constant reminder of the essence of what musicians do. "I went to the club with my dad all the time and I learned what playing guitar was all about and what a jam session really was."

It would be some time before Miller would even admit it to himself that those days sitting in local clubs at the feet of music greats had found its way into his soul. He conceded in a Pop Culture Classics. com interview, "By being around people like Les Paul, Charles Mingus and T-Bone Walker, some really great musicians, I understood from a very early age that this was a profession, a lifetime commitment. And that's what I wanted."

With his family's encouragement and, perhaps most importantly, the presence and influence of Les Paul, Steve, creatively, began to come out of his shell. He would often be found banging out chords on his Gibson and making up primitive songs. It had soon reached a point where the youngster felt he needed an audience other than his immediate family. The neighbourhood kids had no problem hanging out with Steve and listening to him sing and play, usually out of sight in a backyard or a nearby alley. From the perspective of a five-year-old, Steve was quite a good work in progress. So good, in fact, that when George happened upon his son playing and singing one day, he did what he thought was the right and proper thing to do.

He secretly recorded his son and passed the tape on to Les for his assessment. In a 2018 interview that appeared on the website SteveMillerBand.com, Steve recalled the situation with moments of barely disguised rancour.

"The whole tape thing was weird. I was on the second floor of my house, banging on the guitar my uncle had given me. All my little pals were down in the alley behind the house, and I was doing my show. My father snuck upstairs and made a wire recording. I was so mad at him. I was furious that he would sneak into my room and record me like that. It was the first time I had ever heard my voice back and I was totally freaked."

To add insult to Miller's perceived injury, his father, sometime later, gave the tape to Les Paul at a social gathering. Steve protested, telling Paul in no uncertain terms, as quoted in the Milwaukee Journal Sentinel and ThisIsVinylTap.com. "I hated my voice." Paul made Miller an offer no five-year-old could refuse. He would give him a quarter if he let him listen to the tape. The temptation of getting paid for what was Steve Miller's first paying gig proved too much. Steve got his quarter and Les got to hear the tape.

"You've got a great voice," he told the boy. "You can sing and play. You're a musician and you're really going to go places. Just keep practicing."

Abracadabra

Dallas Shock Treatment

To Steve Miller's way of thinking, growing up in Wisconsin was like growing up in the equivalent of the jazz age. It was an important time for Miller. Musically he had his first joys and met some heavy-duty cats. The memories, as he recalled in The Austin Chronicle, ran deep.

"In Wisconsin, we had lots of musician friends. Les Paul and Mary Ford were always around the house. Charles Mingus used to come over a lot. People like that were always at our house at our parties. We lived down the street from the very cool club where everybody used to play and hang out when they were in town."

Those were the thoughts he had as the Miller family packed up the car in 1950 and headed across several state lines to Dallas, Texas, venturing into a region where musical roots, particularly blues, country, and the early stages of rock, marked their journey as they crossed into Texas. The family sensed that they were heading into exciting times. What Miller would reflect on in The Austin Chronicle was that they were heading into a less-than-positive side of human nature.

"This was Dallas in 1950. It was completely segregated. So, when we moved to Texas, it was suddenly like 'what the fuck?' It was like 'What's going on? What's a yankee? What's a rebel?' My father made no bones about the fact that he was a hipster. But our neighbours down the street from where we lived thought we were communists."

It probably did not help the Miller's image in the community when, upon establishing his own pathology lab in Dallas, George saw fit to hire several black technicians, while reestablishing his own recording engineer credentials among the blues clubs and musicians. Needless to say, George Miller's every move seemed to rub the resident segregationists the wrong way. And, in a conversation with The Austin Chronicle some years later, Steve explained how bad it got.

"To give you an idea of what it was like, my father was arrested, handcuffed, and had his picture taken and posted on the front page of The Dallas Morning News for the charge of holding "a race party" at his lab the afternoon before Christmas break. A local state senator,

Ralph Yarborough, stepped in and got the paper to print a retraction. But before that happened, The Dallas Morning News made my father look like some sort of swanky abortion doctor."

"My old man went right downtown and told everybody to go fuck themselves."

T-Bone On The Menu

Steve Miller has never been one to mince words. In fact, the rumour good-naturedly going around for years has been that Miller's nickname was 'cut to the chase'. True or not, that trait was very much in evidence in a conversation with GuitarWorld.com.

"So the next thing I know, we moved to Texas. I was nine years old. T-Bone Walker came over to the house one night and played a party in our living room from 6:00 p.m. to 5:00 a.m. He and my dad became good friends, and he started coming around. He taught me how to play guitar behind my head and things like how to play single note leads."

While meeting and experiencing T-Bone Walker in the visceral was one thing, Miller found much to admire on a personal, spiritual level. His time around Les Paul and Mary Ford was seemingly just the appetiser. He would recall years later in conversation with Steve Miller Band.com that T-Bone was his main dish.

"When he showed up at the house for the first time, I knew he was coming because we rented a piano and the carpet was pulled up. He was just as sharp, clean and beautiful as he could be. As soon as I saw him, I said 'You're T-Bone Walker. Show me. Show me. Show me.' I sat right next to him every time he played and that's how I learned what playing guitar was all about. Being around him, you couldn't help it. It was implanted in my brain."

Even before T-Bone Walker and George Miller became friends and compatriots of the Texas scene, there was a bit of a story to tell. Walker's career in rock and blues encompassed a number of firsts. He was a pioneer in the early stages of electric guitar. One could start a difference of opinion by suggesting that it was Walker, rather than Les Paul, who had plugged in first. A more valid case could be made that Walker's stage antics such as playing guitar behind his head and, reportedly, with his teeth, served as more than a passing influence for the likes of Chuck Berry and, much later, Jimi Hendrix. Musically, Walker had been up, down and all around, and, by the early fifties, was beginning to slow down. Most of his touring had settled in Europe and while he continued to release new music at a fairly steady pace, the overall impact of Walker as a universal presence had begun to wane.

As had his health. Depending on who you talked to, Walker was gradually succumbing to the maladies of age or was a confirmed hypochondriac, in and out of hospitals and doctors' offices complaining of all manner of ailments. In the course of treating what turned out to be a very real ulcer condition, T-Bone and Steve's dad became fast friends, such good buds that, when T-Bone was down on his luck, George would reportedly pay his medical bills.

The tradition started in Milwaukee would continue in Dallas with T-Bone and, on occasion, his backing musicians would regularly swing by the Miller household for a night of playing and recording. And, as had been the case with Les Paul, young Steve would become T Bone's pet and learn some valuable lessons in his odyssey through the blues.

In AntiMusic.Net Steve recalled how Walker took him to guitar school. "T-Bone taught me how to play lead, melodies, how to play guitar behind my head and how to do the splits at the same time. T-Bone teaching me was just amazing."

There were a lot of small moments in his T-Bone education as well, such as the morning he claimed to be feeling unwell so he could stay home from school and watch a late-night concert/jam in the Miller household play to its conclusion. But his T-Bone tutelage would eventually boil down to a very personal, emotional and, most likely spiritual, element that would always linger. It was the sense of community and unabashed creativity that was Steve Miller's signpost and mantra, as he offered in a conversation on The Howard Stern Show and Louder Magazine.

"Watching grown men having a great time doing what they want to do. For me, it was just being there and watching T-Bone play. I would remember that T-Bone would come over again and again and so I have all those memories."

Age Five:
A Musician Until He Dies

Ask Steve Miller a question and he will almost certainly give you an answer. So it seems that prying eyes most likely were asking the wrong questions when it came to particulars; the only thing we seem to know about Miller's school days circa 1950-1956 is that, yes, he did go to school during that period.

A thorough search resulted in bits and pieces. A story in The Dallas Morning News described Miller as "a pint-sized guitarist at Longwood Elementary School." There was also a vague reference and nothing more to the fact that the Miller family moved around a bit in Dallas that referenced Longwood and nothing more.

All the same, it's a safe bet to say that Miller seemed to bounce easily through his second to sixth grade curriculums. He always had the passion of music to balance things out which, within the social circle of pre-teens, made him special. He knew it and he gravitated towards the notion that school was a necessary adjunct to what was really driving him.

Indirectly, Miller's parents were contributing to their son's passions and questions at that relatively early age. All during his early years, Miller's parents continued in their own passion play. They continued to hobnob, hang out and party with all manner of musicians and, for his part, Miller would be right in the middle of it and soaking up the musical vibe and inspiration from the greats. It was all well and good, but the result was that, even at that early age, Miller was expressing to his parents the desire to make music his life. However, Miller recalled in later years with InTheStudio.com that his parents already had non-musical plans for him.

"No one ever thought I would be a professional musician. I was going to go to college, get a degree, get educated and I was going to work. That was the way I was always brought up."

With tongue firmly planted in cheek, in conversation with Pollstar.com, Miller matter-of-factly cut to the chase.

"When I was five-years-old, I wanted to be a musician until I died. I don't know why I understood that or why I wanted to do that.

But I knew I did."

In subsequent interviews, Miller would dance around the question and, in Polstar.com, would lay the lion's share of the credit at his dad's feet. "My dad was a doctor and I worked in his lab at a very young age. But it seemed like I was always around professional musicians. At a young age, I knew that working in a nightclub was serious business. I got a great education when I was young. My dad really sacrificed to get my brother and I into a great school."

St. Marks, Get Set, Go

Miller would turn twelve in 1957. He was the prototypical pre-teen: outgoing, social to the max and basically at a loss as to where life would lead him. Let's walk that last bit of character study back a bit. It continued to be all music, all the time, but it was still largely a creative passion: dreams of a career in music were still unfocused.

But in all honesty, Miller's musical hopes were a dream bordering on something more.

The Miller family remained nomads. George Miller was quite good at pathology and so it was not surprising that better offers would inevitably come his way. Such was the case when a better job necessitated a move that put the family within a short distance of St. Marks School Of Texas, a high-end all-boys college prep institution, cultivated to send its pupils on to a higher career and life standing.

Long story short, St. Marks was a tough and expensive school to get into, but George, with reputation and finances intact, could afford it and it wasn't long before the Miller boys were walking the halls of academia.

Miller quickly found an outlet for his budding creative skills as a member of the St. Marks Boys Choir. "I liked the idea of getting all dressed up and performing," he enthused in The Big Interview. "For me, this was definitely show business."

Beyond general educational requirements, it is not certain which classes Miller was involved in. But by all accounts, every spare moment was devoted to playing the guitar. And that attribute would make him a big man on campus.

"Steve was very outgoing," reflected school chum and fellow musician Bob Haydon in The Dallas Observer. "You might say that he was the life of the classroom and everybody liked him. He was funny and people were kind of drawn to him."

One day in the study hall, fellow student Haydon, as chronicled in his coming-of-age memoir Kensington and The Dallas Observer, suddenly heard some bitching and moaning from another side of the room. It was Steve Miller, who was bemoaning an all-night practice session on his guitar until his fingers nearly bled. Haydon knew that story well. He had spent many similar nights as an aspiring guitarist, listening to surf radio and coming to grips with the specifics of bluegrass music. His fingers had hurt as well, and so he happily turned around and faced this kindred spirit.

For his part, Miller wasted little time in laying his cards on the table. He told Haydon that he was laying plans to form his first band and, in Haydon, saw a possible bandmate. He recounted the conversation in Elsewhere.co.nz. "I told him I was looking to start a band, that I was looking for a rhythm guitar player and did he want to join the band? He said yes."

The pair soon began a series of woodshed practice sessions, the better for Miller and Haydon to get a feel for where each other's creative head was at. Early indications were that Miller's mind was on the blues and Haydon's mind was elsewhere, as was reported in Haydon's book Kensington. Haydon's indoctrination into the way of the blues began when Miller plugged in his electric guitar and played 'Guitar Boogie', a blues instrumental by Arthur Smith. Then it was Haydon's turn who, likewise, plugged in and played 'I Walk The Line' by Johnny Cash. Miller was impressed but not overwhelmed with Haydon's style of music. His response being, "Yeah, but can you play this?" before launching into another oldie but goodie, 'Honky Tonk', a rhythm and blues instrumental courtesy of Bill Doggett. Haydon could, and, in an excerpt from Kensington, realised what the musical direction of the band would be.

When it came to Miller's indoctrination of his new bandmate, Haydon told The Dallas Observer that Miller's approach to teaching was nothing short of 'just do it'. "I had heard 'Honky Tonk' on the radio but had never dreamed of playing it. But Steve showed me and within an hour I was playing backup and he was playing lead."

"Steve was following his own instincts to mould the band his way. He gently steered me away from the stuff I was into and introduced me to the likes of Jimmy Reed and a straight-ahead brand of blues."

The practice sessions continued at a steady pace, incorporating a mixture of blues covers and some forgettable originals. It was too early in the process to call the group anything but An Unnamed Band. But into September 1957, the very first live performance of the very first Steve Miller Band would make an unexpected debut during a shopping trip at Sears Department Store.

Haydon would reflect on the band's unofficial gig in his book Kensington. "One afternoon Steve and I went downtown to a department store to look for new guitars. We found a couple, plugged them into an amp and began playing. We were in the music section on the second floor. But almost immediately a crowd, a lot of them on the first floor, came up and gathered around to watch us play. The music store manager came over. Steve asked if it was okay for us to play and looking at the people we had drawn to his section, he said 'Please! Keep playing!'"

Abracadabra

The Marksmen Open Fire

Things happened pretty quickly after The Unknown Combo's shakedown performance in the department store. For openers, the name Unknown Combo morphed into The Marksmen Combo. In an attempt to fill out a traditional rock and blues sound, Miller recruited another St. Marks classmate, drummer Baron Cass. To Miller's way of thinking they were now a rock and roll band, having put together a smattering of blues covers and originals

Ever the bottom line personality, Miller, when he was not playing or practicing, was already looking for ways to get The Marksmen Combo out there and in the public eye. Being pop culture savvy inspired his approach to playing live, as he told The Dallas Observer. "We felt we could copy the old Ozzie & Harriet TV Show scenario where, at the end of the show, viewers would be transported to a party scene in which Rick and the band would play a few songs. We felt if we could copy that scenario (fifteen-minute musical interludes to break up organised events) we could get some jobs."

The only obstacle was that in 1957, rock and roll was very much in its infancy, as was the market for it in and around Texas. In fact, Miller recalled that the much older and more mature rockers called The Nightcaps were their major source of competition, with the way-ahead-of-their-time mixture of garage rock, hints of psychedelia and blues. People only had a hint of what rock and roll was about and that made getting gigs early on a bit of a chore.

That is, to everyone but Miller, who, when he wasn't playing his music, was deep in thought about how to get gigs. In all honesty, Miller has told this story a million times over the years. You name the outlet and inevitably there was the tale of how The Marksmen got their earliest gigs. But I hold up this live telling during a concert recorded by Sky Cloud Guru as easily one of the most colourful and telling of the times.

"There was rock and roll on the radio but there weren't any rock and roll bands in the city of Dallas and we were determined to make The Marksmen a growing business. So I wrote up some letters and sent them to schools, sororities, churches, synagogues, any place that might want a band for their party. We would be charging seventy-five dollars for a gig and we would be booking shows for the next three weeks for the rest of the school semester. So I would be sitting at home and the phone would ring. Some people would complain that seventy-five dollars was a lot of money and I would tell them 'Well that's the going rate' and click, hang up on them. A lot of them would inevitably call back in a bit and agree to the terms. In no time at all The Marksmen would be booked up for shows every Friday and Saturday through the rest of the year. I was able to get my mother to drive us to the early gigs because we were all too young to drive. A lot of those shows would be playing for wild drunken sorority parties and they didn't even realise that we were only twelve. We wore dark glasses and had on ties to make us look older. Those first shows we played a lot of blues, things like Bobby Bland and Jimmy Reed and it went down really well. We were always playing."

The reason The Marksmen Combo were always playing was that Miller was decidedly hard when it came to negotiating the gigs. An attitude he was quick to point out in conversation with the magazine Ultimate Classic Rock. "I don't know why I was that way at age twelve. But I didn't want to hear anybody's sad story. My price was fair."

The early days of The Marksmen Combo's existence were looked upon with no small amount of amusement by those who saw teen bands as a traditional rite of passage before real life, family and responsibility set in. Miller heard it all and, in The Aspen Times, chose to ignore the doubters. "Most people would say 'well isn't that cute?'. But we played every weekend at country clubs, churches and fraternities. And when we weren't playing, I was on the phone booking gigs all the time."

The Marksmen's first year as a performing group was, not unexpectedly, centred around Dallas area schools and related activities, the most sublime being their first paying gig, a twelve-year-old neighbour's birthday party, for which the band members received five dollars each. Their first show of any consequence was a local dance studio get-together at a church with more than one-hundred excited teens in attendance. What would qualify as their biggest break to date was when a local brand of the Neiman Marcus fashion brand asked The Marksmen to play at a teen fashion show at the hip local hangout, the Zodiac Room. Band member Haydon would remember that show well in his memoir Kensington (71). "Word of our popularity had spread around the local schools, and we were surprised when Neiman Marcus asked us to play. At the end of the performance a crowd of girls gathered around us and asked for booking information."

The band's popularity would result in their first brush with big name stardom when they were hired to open for the annual Junior Symphony Ball which top-lined no lesser light than Neil Sedaka.

Through the end of 1957 and well into 1958, The Marksmen Combo was beginning to feel their oats. Nobody was more cocksure of their popularity and their potential for something big than Miller, who, as chronicled in Bruno Cerotti's look at Steve Miller's early days, captured a moment when Miller's ego was very much front and centre.

"We had this very cool band and a bunch of guys really dug the band. When we showed up and played, the place moved. We weren't just some bullshit band. There's not a nightclub in the land we couldn't have paralysed."

Members of the band were most certainly feeling it when they let their enthusiasm fly in a Dallas Observer article. Miller said, "Everywhere we played was fantastically exciting. A hundred kids would rush the stage to hear us playing a fifteen-minute set." Haydon was philosophical but no less caught up in the moment when he said, "It gave you chills up and down. The thing about being that age is that you're fearless, and that all the girls are leaning in, looking at you and smiling, and you could just feel it. They just loved it. It was a real exciting time." Miller reverted to teen form when he told The Dallas Morning News, "We were insufferable. By the time we would reach age fifteen we would all be rich."

In The Dallas Observer, drummer Baron Cass would echo all the previous sentiments before offering a much deeper caveat. "We were rich from playing so much. But we were also rich in other ways too."

Abracadabra

Evolution On The March

It would be crass and downright insulting to describe The Marksmen Combo as Steve Miller and a bunch of guys named Moe. But in all honesty, shortly after the formation of the band, that's exactly what the situation was. Miller recruited all the band members, in some cases he taught them how to play the instruments, he drew up the set and song lists and, perhaps most important of all in those early days, he did the business of getting the gigs and making sure everybody got paid. All the rest of the band had to do was show up on time and play.

Not so fast.

The evolution of The Marksmen Combo was, for Miller, an exercise in the young man finding his footing musically in the world. The always-candid Miller would acknowledge in Vulture.com that, initially, The Marksmen Combo was taking baby steps. "At that point it was kind of three chords and some blues songs. It was all pretty simple and straightforward."

Miller, night after night, was moving slowly but surely away from the prevailing musical form of old-style country blues to modern electric guitar rock. "T-Bone was the bridge for me," Miller offered in Polstar.com. Haydon, who had a nightly front row seat to where the band was at and going, recalled in The Dallas Observer and his memoir Kensington what he witnessed as The Marksmen Combo becoming the hot band on the block.

"We weren't simply playing for what passed for regular rock and roll. What we were doing was more blues influenced, like Jimmy Reed, B.B. King and Muddy Waters. What we were doing was a return to Steve's roots, his time sitting at the feet of Les Paul and T-Bone Walker. It was everything he had heard channelled into a rock and roll beat."

As the proverbial leader of the pack, Miller was prone to making impulsive and calculating decisions, which often entailed situations both amusing and real. When getting rides to their gigs was beginning to get problematic, Miller decided that they needed a bass player, recruited his older brother, taught him to play bass and to become the driver to gigs because he was the only one old enough to have a driver's license. As they moved up the ladder from local high school gigs, the question remained of how they could pass for older than they were. Even though nobody ever thought to question their age, Miller began outfitting the group with glasses and ties to make them appear older.

Miller would have a good laugh at the age situation during The Big Interview. "We went through all that stuff to make us seem older. We never mentioned how old we were and nobody ever mentioned it."

During that same interview, Miller matter-of-factly acknowledged that into 1958, stylistically, it was time for a pivotal moment in his musical development. "For the first six months we were doing nothing but instrumentals. Then the band got together and I said, 'Well I've got to sing something.' So I started to sing."

Eventually The Marksmen Combo evolved into a band that needed more bottom sound. When his brother Buddy got out of the band to get married and live a more secure life, Miller took it upon himself to expand the lineup as only Miller could, which was to find fellow classmates, walk up to them and see if they wanted to join a band. It was the prototypical Steve Miller recruiting pitch that landed classmate Rodger Gaulding on double duty as vocalist and harmonica player. But easily the most significant and well-known addition to the band courtesy of The St. Marks minor league system would be Boz Scaggs, who would survive stints in The Marksmen Combo, the early incarnation of The Steve Miller Band, and finally, a wide ranging solo career right up to the present. Miller remembered the feeling out process in On Wisconsin Magazine as well as in an endless number of interviews over the years.

"Boz and I went to the same school. I had started The Marksmen Combo in the seventh grade. By the eighth grade I decided to ask Boz to join the band. Boz was a year behind me in school." Justifying adding Scaggs to the group necessitated another on-the-job training session on the guitar, being taught by Miller who would become a triple threat on bass, vocals and enough chords on the guitar to qualify as a fully-fledged Marksmen.

Historically, the meeting between Scaggs and Miller and his joining The Marksmen Combo has been fragmentary at best. Scaggs, musically, had been on a voyage of discovery, his most significant accomplishment to that point had been as part of a folk orientated group called The Bacchanal Trio, who appeared for a time in Dallas area clubs doing their Kingston Trio thing. Between the two of them, the origin of how Scaggs and Miller got together remains vague at best.

Scaggs explained to Rolling Stone that "Meeting Steve Miller was maybe the most important thing that happened to me to that point." Miller would add a bit more when talking to On Wisconsin Magazine when he acknowledged "Boz and I went to the same school. In the eighth grade I asked Boz if he wanted to join The Marksmen Combo. I taught him some blues guitar licks and he ended up singing some vocals. It was as simple as that."

Well into 1958, the now-realigned-into-a-solid five-piece The Marksmen Combo had plateaued. The shows were now much longer and venturing into the more lucrative college fraternity and club scene outside the limits of Dallas. Miller would recall in VintageGuitar.com that the repertoire was also expanding. "We were definitely working. We were doing the rhythm and blues and rock numbers then we started doing Motown stuff. It was a lot of fun times."

All of which was increasingly focused on Miller, whose passion on guitar was real and emotionally driven. Even if listeners were not totally into the music, they could not help but recognise the legitimacy of Miller as a musician who walked the walk. Years later, George Thorogood, someone many have considered a contemporary, heaped praise on Miller on his website GeorgeThorogood.com. "All you have to do is listen to Steve Miller's guitar. You know he listened to Freddy King. You know he listened to Johnny 'Guitar' Watson and a lot of people. You know he put in the time and learned that style of music."

During the formative development of The Marksmen Combo, Miller fell in love with Jimmy Reed who emerged as the youngster's be-all and end-all. "I had started listening to Jimmy Reed when I was eleven years old," he said in Joenickp.Blogspot. "I was just absolutely sucked in. The tunes were so cool. The playing was so loose."

Miller's infatuation with Reed culminated when he was around fourteen years old, during the opportunity to play backup for a series of Jimmy Reed shows in clubs in and around the Dallas area, including Lou Ann's Bar.

Miller would be awed speechless when playing for this major influence in his life. "What can I say?" he told VintageGuitar.com. "I was fourteen. I had my own band. And we were backing Jimmy Reed. It didn't get any better than that."

Abracadabra

Miller's Out Of Here

That Steve Miller would quite naturally gravitate towards music and the not-too-veiled notion of making a living at it, was probably not that much of a surprise. After all, in the best possible way, his parents had created the monster. By the time their personable son formed The Marksmen Combo, there was equal parts pride and amusement as they watched their son make his early attempts at music a career.

They were alternately amused when their son would dodge the ten o'clock nightly curfew, they had set for him to book gigs on the phone. They were amused and surprisingly agreeable to have his mother driving the band to and from gigs because none of the band members had a driver's license. It went without saying they were amazed when, a year into The Marksmen Combo odyssey, their son, barely twelve at the time, would loudly proclaim that he was making three-hundred dollars a month off his music.

They would be less than thrilled when Miller, as well as band member Bob Haydon, was kicked out of St. Marks in his junior year. Miller would casually acknowledge the incident in years and interviews to come that included The Dallas Observer. "They (the school administration) felt that Bob and I did not represent the school in a positive way because we were in a band and they did not like rock and roll. They didn't care for rock and roll and I had real long hair."

School Administrator David W. Dini, while generally expressing favour towards Miller's attitude in both The Living Church and Texas Monthly, offered a mild addendum to Miller's account of what happened. "To be clear, Steve did not graduate from St. Marks because right before his senior year, he got expelled for having a bad attitude and for running an underground newspaper."

How Miller's parents reacted to the news remains a mystery; extensive research could not produce a single comment on the matter. Reading between the lines, as well as the fact that he immediately enrolled at Woodrow Wilson High School for his senior year, it is plausible that there had been some kind of 'come to Jesus' moment between parents and son, and that if any conditions were laid down, it had been that Miller, his overriding feelings about music aside, needed to graduate from high school with a diploma.

Consequently, Miller's senior year at Woodrow Wilson High School would go by with little to no notice outside of a short item in the school newspaper that highlighted his athletic prowess in track and field. However, the steady climb to graduation in the Class Of 1961 was noted by the fact that The Marksmen Combo continued to gig.

At least for a couple of months after Miller graduated. As it turned out, June to September 1961 would be The Marksmen Combo's swan song, at least with Miller in the band. Miller, most likely as a relief to his parents, had decided to go to college at The University of Wisconsin and major in comparative literature and creative writing. By the way he would describe it in On Wisconsin Magazine, Miller's decision to go to UW was typically Miller. "I had a cousin there. I had friends there. I had an older brother who had come to UW for a summer school session and came back with a glowing report. The school had a wonderful reputation and great History and English departments. But the main thing was that it was really far away from home."

"And I wanted to get the hell out of town."

Steve Miller Is In All The Bands

Miller arrived at the University of Wisconsin campus in September 1961, excited to really be on his own for the first time. A few people knew him from his days in The Marksmen Combo but, as of three months prior, that band and its regional notoriety were in the wind. On the surface, Miller was just another largely faceless student, going about his business in Comparative Literature classes.

However, the musical aspirations were far from gone. Despite the fact that he was totally without a band, his urge to musically merge was there in spades and, in that sense, he was all ego and arrogance as he began to check out the local music scene in and around the campus. Ken Adamany, a fellow UW student as well as a keyboardist in a frat house band called The Knightranes, would see the ID in Miller up close and personal, as he recalled in a Washington Post conversation.

"We were playing a frat party and Steve stood right up front during our set. He came up to me afterwards and introduced himself. He said, 'I'm Steve Miller from Dallas and I'm looking to get into a band. I play guitar, bass, harmonica and sing. And I'm better than everyone in your band. Including you'."

Adamany realised the outrageousness of the encounter, but would insist in the same conversation, "That was his actual quote. And you know something, he was right."

In typical Miller musical fashion, the young student immediately proved all talk and all action. He quickly got the lay of the land and found a niche that he was quite happy to fill, as he recalled in The Washington Post. "When I went up to the University of Wisconsin, I found that they didn't have any bands except for dance bands. So I started a rock and roll band."

The inception of The Ardells was a Steve Miller blueprint. He recruited his band from the UW community. When Jos Davidson showed potential, Miller sat him down and taught him how to play rhythm guitar. Also on board what would be the first incarnation of The Ardells, was Brian Friedman (piano) and Ronnie Boyer (drums). Between September 1961 and June 1962, The Ardells, playing what Miller would often describe as 'Texas-style shuffle blues', played primarily the university party circuit, the occasional local club appearance, and a couple of small-scale concerts. The Ardells itinerary dovetailed easily with Miller's academic life, in which he was quite enthusiastic about the notion of literature and writing.

When the summer vacation rolled around, there was Miller, Boyd, and a revolving group of musicians in a reconstituted version of The Knightranes. It was the equivalent of a summer vacation for Miller: a free and easy way to play out, turn a buck, and expand their sphere of influence with a number of shows in Illinois, as well as their stronghold of Wisconsin. Occasionally, members would be late for a gig and a suitable replacement would be found. The approach worked fine with Miller and was in the tradition of 'the show must go on'.

With the end of summer, Miller returned to the University of Wisconsin and, not surprisingly, discovered that half of The Ardells had graduated or moved on to greener pastures. Miller was not too upset. He just got out his list of people and said, 'Well I wonder what Boz Scaggs is up to these days?'

As it turned out, Scaggs had recently graduated from St. Marks and was casting about for higher education. Miller was soon on the phone, extolling the virtues of UW campus life and, 'oh by the way, I've got another band called The Ardells, do you still play bass?' Scaggs did a quick study on the kind of music The Ardells were playing and was soon part and parcel of the band whose reputation proceeded it and it was not long before The Ardells were back to regularly playing.

"We played a lot," Miller remembered in an interview with On Wisconsin. "We played all the parties, the sorority parties, all the dorm parties, just everything. We usually played five times a weekend. In the afternoon we'd play the beer suppers, we'd play a fraternity before the football game and after the football game."

Pianist Ben Sidran, an introspective jazz musician, recounted in his autobiography, A Life In The Music, how one afternoon, as he was driving through the campus on his motorbike, he heard The Ardells playing a style of music that deeply resonated with him. "I heard a four-piece band playing a rocking groove. The music they were playing was rough, urban with no intellectual pretensions, just good old animal magnetism. And the clincher was that they had no piano player."

That situation would not last long, because after a short feeling out process, Sidran would find himself a full member of The Ardells, and involved in all the rock and roll craziness that would entail. Of course, craziness all depended on who you talked to. Ardell's drummer Ronnie Boyer, in a quote excerpted by rock historian Bruno Ceriotti found it to be a good-natured gas. "The jobs on campus in the fall, during football season and before and after the games, were always a riot. The beer was flowing and everybody was getting pretty nuts. Those were great parties. Everybody danced and everybody had fun. They were easy jobs. Everybody was in love with the band because we did such different things."

Sidran, in his memoir A Life in the Music took a more measured, somewhat practical approach to The Ardells' experience. "At that time I was making thirty-five dollars a night when I was leading my own little jazz trio. When I joined The Ardells, I often got fifty dollars a night just to have a ball."

Miller's workaholic nature was much in evidence during 1962 and 1963. It seemed that The Marksmen Combo and Knightranes was not enough to scratch the itch, even though one could easily put an asterisk by any Miller appearances. According to an 18th July 1962 flyer for a Knightranes show, Steve Miller was listed as 'formerly with The Fireballs, Dallas Texas'. No other mention of The Fireballs was forthcoming, so it is essentially a fabrication of an overzealous promoter. But like all good mysteries, it remains to be seen.

A more tangible report, complete with an eyewitness account, had a gig billed as Steve Miller and his New Music as taking place in Madison, Wisconsin. According to singer-songwriter Nick Gravenites, in a quote excerpted by rock historian Bruno Ceriotti, this one shot of Steve Miller and his New Music went down like this: "When it was time for Steve's show, he came on stage with three guitars, two tape recorders and a microphone. He started up the tape recorders, which played pre-recorded tracks, and he picked up his guitar and started to play and sing all by his lonesome."

Miller was always a mischievous sort who could seemingly find a dark sense of humour and irony in just about any situation. Such was the case in 1963 when Miller took the opportunity to take over another band's identity and actually follow through with the gig. Ben Sidran was there when it happened and had a blast, recalling it in his book A Life In The Music. "Joe Baldwin, a local singer who had booked the gig for his own band, The Diablos, had double booked himself that night. So Steve and I and some other guys (whose names had long since passed into obscurity) drive the hundred miles to the Chicago suburb and a Northwestern University frat party and pretended to be Joe Baldwin and The Diablos. We carried our own instruments up a ladder into the loft of a barn where the fraternity brothers had cleared out a space for a dance floor and set up next to a huge tub of white lightning. Before the night was over, some of the sorority sisters had misplaced their clothes and some of the brothers had fallen out of the loft. Because of what happened when we played, the real Joe Baldwin and The Diablos were forever banned from Northwestern University."

Name: Steve Miller.
Occupation: Radical.

The University of Wisconsin: Everybody who entered its hallowed halls of higher education had their reasons. Steve Miller certainly had his. If only he could figure out what they were. Mentions of his time at UW have been fragmented at best, and slanted at worst.

Here's what we do know:

Miller was slotted into Contemporary Literature and the writing life. But most of the ink spilled in the seven semesters and the one semester trip abroad at the University of Copenhagen came across as afterthoughts, a stop-gap in Miller's odyssey into music. For Miller, his years at the University of Wisconsin were an emotional tug of war. He was a liberal from the word go thanks to his parental upbringing, cautiously rooted in all political and social causes – especially when it came to those early musical aspirations, as he acknowledged in Loudersound.com. "When I started in music, I figured what I was into would change the world. The thing for me was to transcend entertainment and deal with important issues."

From a non-music point of view, Miller was also finding much that turned him on in terms of contemplating literature, all the great writers that teased his creative mind. "The more writers you read, the broader your thinking becomes," he reported in On Wisconsin Magazine. "That was a big part of it for me. It broadened my vision and my ability to write."

Miller's parents were most certainly heartened to hear things like that because, truth be known, while they were quite thrilled with their son's musical achievements to that point, they were hoping that, for security's sake, he would ultimately choose a more academic, studious lifestyle. And for a time, Miller seemed to be wrestling with his options. He told TomWriteTurns.com: "I was planning on being a teacher of literature and creative writing. But I quickly found out that I was more serious about music than about teaching."

This brought Miller full circle. Whether anybody cared to admit it, The Ardells, during his tenure at the University of Wisconsin, was marked by a lot of rock and roll. Miller ticked off gigs in ClassicRock.

com. "It was gigs at fraternity houses, gigs at dorms on the lawns. We were a great band. We did a lot of blues, Motown stuff, The Rolling Stones. We were the hot band on campus."

Like many students of the time, Miller became a social and political radical, throwing himself actively into the deep end of the extreme issues of the day. As he explored in conversation with On Wisconsin Magazine, when activism entered his life, he found himself participating in a brave new world of involvement.

"The things I really learned at college were when I joined The Student Non-Violent Coordinating Committee (SNCC) and became a Freedom Rider in the civil rights movement. I was also involved in the anti-war movement. That was probably the greatest thing I was exposed to in college. That there were activists on the campus and it wasn't something you just read about. If you felt as I did, very disturbed by the condition of blacks in America, and you wanted to fight for civil rights, that was the important part for me. It was more the political atmosphere on the campus than it actually was the classes that I was taking."

For Miller, the decision to get actively involved would also have its philosophical downside. He conceded in LouderSound.com, "The closer I got to people like Jerry Rubin and The Yippie Movement, the less I liked them. The further I got into radicalism, the more I realised the people running those things weren't that great. In fact, they became as unpleasant as the people on the extreme right, and for a liberal like me, that was bad news."

Miller would be deep and thoughtful when it came to the prevailing political and social times. After music, what was going on in the world and what he could do about it was uppermost in his mind, especially on the occasion of his turning eighteen and he received a missive from Uncle Sam requesting his presence. "It was a dark time," remembered Miller in LouderSound.com. "The government was running The Vietnam War. It was like 'you're eighteen, you're next, off you go.' "

Needless to say, Miller did not want to go and, in the same LouderSound.com interview, he explained how he came up with a clever way out of it. He showed up at his army enrolment board with a tape of crazy, incomprehensible electronic music in tow. It would have the desired effect on the draft board. "They told me 'the army doesn't want you Mr. Miller. You will either end up in jail or you would screw up an entire division'."

"My work was done."

Steve Hits Chicago...
Chicago Hits Back

By September 1964, the handwriting between Steve Miller and music was on shaky ground.

In September 1963, Miller had officially quit The Ardells. During the summer break, he also called it quits with The Knightranes. Miller slipped into creative isolation. He recalled in his conversation with Isthmus.com, "I really started at the end of my time in Madison. I had listened to a lot of different writers. I was young. I was talented. I could play and write good music and had some fairly good ideas. But as time goes on, you learn a lot as you grow up."

What Miller would learn fairly quickly would lead to the onset of insecurity and depression, as he admitted with no small amount of angst in conversation with Vintage Guitar Magazine. "Suddenly I didn't think there was a future for me in music. It was the first time I wasn't in a band since I was twelve years old and I really didn't like it. I'd go to see bands, go to festivals and concerts and I couldn't sit in with anybody because everybody was real protective about his stage time and didn't want to share."

Entering his senior year at University of Wisconsin, with his sense of a music life slipping away, Miller would opt for a semester overseas at the University of Copenhagen, Denmark, to study literature and creative writing. He was resigned to where this creative choice would take him, as he said in Mix.com. "I thought I was going to get a master's degree, a doctorate and then become a teacher because there was always this pressure on me to get a real job."

Miller finally succumbed, willingly, to the devil he knew and desired. Halfway through his time in Copenhagen, he was a mere six credits away from graduating from UW with a degree when he left Europe and came back to the States. Making his way back to Dallas, Miller made an emotional and spiritual pit-stop in the home of the blues, Chicago. He hung out, hit the clubs, and one night, was captivated by The Paul Butterfield Blues Band in a dark and smoky club. The temptation of the Windy City had won out.

Now came the tough part.

It didn't take long for Miller to rationalise his decision, as he reflected in Mix.com. "After one year in Europe, I came back home and everything looked different to me. Comparative Literature was just no fun at all. I really didn't want to teach Creative Writing and Comparative Literature. It all seemed like bullshit."

It would not seem like bullshit when George and Bertha Miller came to the University of Wisconsin campus and Miller laid it on the line. He would wince at the memory in Vintage Guitar Magazine. "About the time I realised that I really didn't want to do anything else but music, I had the conversation with my mom and dad. They asked, 'What are you gonna do?'. I told them, 'What I really want to do is go to Chicago and play blues.' My father had spent a lot of money on my college education and, at that moment he gave me the look that said if he had a two-by-four, he would hit me with it. But my mother said, 'I think that's a great idea. You're young. You don't have any responsibility'."

"I left the next day for Chicago."

But not before he received a phone call from Nick Gravenites, who had been in the audience when Miller had done his New Music act and had been impressed with his blues and experimental ways. Gravenites, who was then part of the Chicago blues scene and about to open a music orientated bar called The Burning Bush, recalled in a BluesPower.blog, "I called Steve in Dallas and told him that my partner and I were opening a new music bar in Chicago and asked him if he wanted to come and play any kind of music he wanted."

Miller took him up on his offer and quickly recruited some likeminded, imaginative band mates and The World War Three Blues Band hit the ground running at The Burning Bush. Little has been chronicled about the short-lived The World War Three Blues Band other than their propensity for humour, imagination and talent. The band played around sporadically into the summer of 1965 before breaking up, but it would prove a first step for Miller into the Chicago Blues scene which, in many cases, was like the wild, wild west, populated by such legendary gunslingers as Howlin Wolf, Muddy Waters, Buddy Guy and Junior Wells. As the new kid on the block, Miller quickly learned how the game was played, as he recalled in Vintage Guitar Magazine, For Bass Players Only, and SteveMillerBand. com.

"I spent three years in Chicago and I learned that if you weren't on top of your game, Junior Wells or somebody else would steal your gig. In Chicago, there were like five nightclubs and six bands. So, it was not uncommon that I was trying to get Howlin' Wolf's gig while he was trying to get my gig while I was trying to get his gig."

Miller would also discover that to play the blues game in Chicago was to deal with some tough customers who were running the show. "In Chicago, the scene was basically a bunch of gangsters who were running the nightclubs, there was payola with club owners and the cops. But this was a time when the blues artists' records weren't selling really well and they had to do what they had to do to make a living, and so the gangsters were stealing from the musicians. It was a very hot scene. It was a blues scene."

Abracadabra

Hanging With The Fishes

Steve Miller was nothing if not a quick study. He would constantly harken back to those coming-of-age days in Chicago as his graduation diploma for his life as a musician. "I spent some time in Chicago with a lot of mature men," he reflected in a conversation with Vulture.com. "It was an important period for me."

Although he continued to learn from the legends of the genre, he also kept his ear to the ground when it came to what was happening in the rest of the world. And what he had been hearing was a lot of things starting to happen, musically, in San Francisco.

There was the early stage of musical evolution going on. The scene in and around the Bay Area was embryonic. What were considered hippie musicians were few and far between, and the term 'psychedelic' was only whispered about in dark corners. In the backwash of increasing political and social activism and free this and free that, Miller, in a Vulture.com interview, went on to enthuse of those early impressions. "The time I spent in San Francisco and the Bay Area was a very experimental time. You could do anything you wanted to do. Anything."

Miller ended up in Berkeley, the university town that was just coming into its own as the centre of the political and social universe. He quickly assimilated into the bohemian world when he moved into a communal house populated by a struggling and often starving group of musicians. Among those drifting in and out were two notables, Joe McDonald and Barry Melton, who were just on the cusp of notoriety as founding members of Country Joe and The Fish.

The house was situated behind a coffee shop/folk music club called The Jabberwock. Given the often unpredictable climate of the times, the owner of the The Jabberwock would often find himself without any live entertainment and would wander over to the house to ask if anybody was interested in doing a set. Thus was born an informal group called The Instant Action Jug Band, an ever-evolving group of musicians including, on occasion, Miller, who would walk over and play. As excerpted from the book Eight Miles High: Folk Rock From Haight Ashbury to Woodstock by Richie Uttenburger, commune member and future fish Barry Melton gave insight into how the whole give-and-take exchange worked.

"We lived mostly on white bread, peanut butter, powdered skimmed milk and any leftovers we could scrounge after the customers ate. The exchange was fair, at least from a starving musician's point of view."

Miller's participation in The Instant Action Jug Band was fragmentary at best. What is known is that between September and October 1965, he would occasionally sit in with the band and, perhaps more importantly, soak up the early stages of where the music was heading. He liked what he saw and heard, and it was a scene that he had a strong desire to be a part of.

But at the end of the day, Miller was a realist who still had musical and psychological ties to what passed for some semblance of a steady gig on the blues scene.

And so it was not long before Miller was on his way back to the Windy City.

Miller, Goldberg, Hullabullo, Goodbye

The blues. Nothing predictable about it. Don't take my word for it. The blues in 1965 was a surprise waiting to happen. Just ask Barry Goldberg, who remembered the time with BluesPower.blog. "I was walking down the street in Chicago when I heard this amazing guitar playing coming out of a storefront. I ran in and it was Steve Miller. As it turned out, Paul Butterfield was ending his stint at the cool club Big Johns (the better to sign a big label deal with Elektra Records) and they needed a new band. I asked Steve if he wanted to join forces and audition for the gig. We did, and we got the gig and it would last about a year. We had the magic together."

The Miller Goldberg Band, which also included bassist Roy Ruby and drummer Maurice McKinley, almost immediately became one of the most in-demand bands at Big John's, as well as up and down Chicago's vaunted North Side. Like all top-notch bands, The Miller Goldberg Band was professional, tight and musically adept at covers as well as originals. Word on the scene was that Miller/Goldberg were not too far away from a record deal.

While the band played a non-stop storm all over Chicago, Miller also found time to occasionally sit in with the big boys and, as he related in Vintage Guitar Magazine, just be a fan. "I got to see Buddy Guy at least a hundred times and Howlin' Wolf at least fifty times. Big Johns was where you went to see all the big guys. I learned a lot."

However, the hammerlock that the unscrupulous club owners and managers had on the scene was such that financially, Miller was still a pauper. He ruefully recalled in Vintage Guitar Magazine, "Playing in Chicago, I was making one-hundred-and-twenty-five dollars a week, working from 9:00 p.m. to 4:00 a.m., six days a week. It was enough money to rent a room, eat, buy a car, and maybe pay for insurance on the car."

The Miller Goldberg Blues Bands' luck would take an unexpected turn. During a meet, greet and play music industry convention in Chicago, the band came to the attention of Epic Records, who signed them. The band were immediately thrown into the rock and roll rat race when they were given a day-and-a-half of studio time. It resulted in ten songs for an album called Blowing My Mind. Two singles from the album, 'The Mother Song' and 'More Soul Than Soulful', did only so-so in terms of business, but the buzz surrounding the band was such that The Miller Goldberg Blues Band were invited to Manhattan, where they were asked to play the television music show Hullabaloo, opposite The Four Tops and The Supremes.

Miller was gob-smacked by these first hints of popular acceptance on a much bigger scale than the Chicago blues circuit. Blowing My Mind was his first real recording experience, and the lightning-fast pace and logistics of the process were eye openers, as was the Hullabaloo appearance and the first brushes with big city media coverage. The vibe continued positively as The Miller Goldberg Blues Band were immediately linked to a band in a residence gig at the popular New York night spot The Phone Booth.

Following their time on the east coast, the band returned to Chicago where, for Miller, the good cheer had suddenly gone sour, as he painfully recalled in Vintage Guitar Magazine. "When we got back to Chicago, it was like the whole scene had left town. Everybody had gotten successful and didn't have to play the blues clubs anymore. They were all playing the east coast and the west coast and playing college shows and concerts and making fifteen-hundred dollars a night. The whole scene in Chicago had dried up. So as fast as I could, I wanted to get out of the nightclub business and into the rock and roll concert business."

Never far from a dramatic gesture, Miller's final decision on where to go was based on the toss of a coin, as he remembered in USA Today. "I flipped a coin to see if I would drive east to New York or to the city that was seemingly always on my mind. There was a pulse about it, as if I could put my ear to a railroad track that said 'here was San Francisco'."

Miller's emotional coin pointed west.

As chronicled in the Sweetwater.com podcast, Miller left The Miller Goldberg Band and made his way in a very-used VW Microbus with rapidly dwindling funds to San Francisco. He got there with exactly five dollars to his name. The Fillmore had a show headlining Paul Butterfield and the first show by the Jefferson Airplane featuring new singer Grace Slick. Miller spent his last five dollars on a ticket.

Miller remembered that at one point in Butterfield's set, his good buddy spotted him in the audience and asked him to come up and jam with the band. Miller jumped on stage and did a couple of numbers with Paul and the band. He was so caught up in the magic of being in San Francisco and the moment of essentially playing his first Fillmore show that, when Butterfield introduced Miller to the audience, Miller's mouth got the best of him, as he jokingly related in Sweetwater.com.

"I yelled out that I was Steve Miller and that I was the leader of The Steve Miller Band and that they would be hearing from us real soon. The Fillmore audience cheered. There was only one problem with what I said. There was no actual Steve Miller Band at that point."

"I was it."

Abracadabra

You Need To Come Here Now

For the sake of credibility, Miller knew immediately that he would quickly need to assemble a real Steve Miller Blues Band. That's when he did what he always did in a pinch. He called home.

As chronicled in RockProspography101.com and TheStrangeBrew.com, Miller called up old friends and musicians Curly Cooke (guitar) and Tim Davis (drums), (and, for all you completists, Dick Presonett (bass), who would only last a few gigs before homesickness set in and he returned to Wisconsin).

The Steve Miller Blues Band immediately went into serious practice mode and over the Thanksgiving holidays in 1966, learned a total of twenty-five songs – equivalent to a good two sets in most clubs. In RockProspography101.com, Miller would give his seal of approval when he said, "the band learned twenty-five songs and they were in-tune and tight."

The Steve Miller Blues Band made their debut performance at the Berkeley coffee house, The Forum on 2nd December 1966. By all accounts, the performance, primarily consisting of covers of classic and obscure blues/rock covers, was promising. Word of mouth resulted in the band headlining at The Matrix for four dates with opening acts Steve Mann and the Congress Of Wonders.

Again, word of mouth on the band's The Matrix appearances was good. Unfortunately, the band collectively (and Miller in particular) was running low on cash. Miller, at one point, was seriously thinking about going back to Chicago. Fortunately, in the sixties music pecking order, The Steve Miller Blues Bands' stock had risen; a two-night stand at The Avalon Ballroom in late December, as opening act for The Grateful Dead and Moby Grape, resulted in a cash payout of five-hundred dollars. It was enough for Miller to celebrate by renting a small Berkeley apartment and treating the band to dinner and a movie.

Miller quickly grasped the business and practical aspects as he neared the end of his initial journey, learning firsthand about the challenges of navigating the music scene during the hippie era with its unconventional band names. He was also downright philosophical in USA Today about what this pivotal moment in musical time meant to him. "The sixties was such a cool, small scene. The group of people who started this scene were idealistic in a period of time that wasn't cynical. It was all about the art."

Into the new year, and an early January two-night stand at The Avalon Ballroom opening for the Quicksilver Messenger Service, The Steve Miller Blues Band was moving along nicely with nary a stumble. When bassist Dick Personett took that moment to leave the band, Miller barely missed a beat in hiring Berkeley resident Lonnie Turner, whom he had met on his previous trip to the Bay Area, as a replacement. And when Miller decided that the band needed a fuller sound that could only be supplied by an organ player, he once again called home, as keyboard player Jim Peterman recalled in an interview with TheStrangeBrew.com.

"I was still in college at the University of Wisconsin. We all knew each other, so when they decided they wanted to add a keyboard player for the sound, they called and offered to fly me out in February '67 to play for the weekend and see how we all felt about it. That was a very exciting weekend in my life. We just played (at Miller's house) and just jammed for about ten hours."

Peterman flew back to the University of Wisconsin and resumed his studies. The decision on his joining The Steve Miller Blues Band was still up in the air. But the band would be far from idle over the next month, making regular appearances at The Avalon Ballroom, The Matrix, The Fillmore and a couple of short hops to Vancouver British Columbia and Los Angeles to appear in multi band festivals. In the meantime, Peterman was still on the hook, as he reported in TheStrangeBrew.com. "When they did call back, they said, 'Yeah, we'd love to have you and we think it's going to sound good, but you really need to come here now.' But I really had to sort that one out. I called back and said, 'I'm three months away from graduating from school after five years. If you can wait for me, I'd appreciate it.' And they decided to wait. Thank goodness."

Peterman finally pulled the trigger in late May of 1967 and hopped on a plane to San Francisco to join Miller and the band. Peterman was thrilled at the prospects, but his attitude would do a one-eighty by the time his plane touched down.

"I was scared shitless," he told TheStrangeBrew.com. "I didn't think I was an adequate player and I was being dropped right in the middle of this incredible event."

Monterey Pop: The Miller Report

An incredible event, the forerunner of Woodstock and countless other monsters of rock festivals, the Monterey International Pop Festival played out over three days and nights over 16th-18th June 1967 at the Monterey County Fairgrounds in Northern California. To many observers, this grand experiment was a bit of a roll of the dice. Thirty-three of the biggest international musicians, including The Who, The Jimi Hendrix Experience, Ravi Shankar, and an impressive lineup of Bay Area bands and musicians such as Big Brother & The Holding Company, The Grateful Dead, Country Joe & The Fish, and The Quicksilver Messenger Service, participated in the event.

For The Steve Miller Blues Band, performing a tight forty-minute set of hard-driving blues in an afternoon slot during day two of the festival, it was a bit of a coming-out as they played in front of the largest audience they had experienced to date. Band member Peterman reflected in TheStrangeBrew.com (that he still had a bit of the jitters despite having rounded into shape with a couple of warm-up shows in out-of-the-way bars, moments before stepping out on stage. "It was scary. We had practiced. We were tight. But when it came right down to it, yeah, it scared the shit out of me."

For his part, Miller served as a post-festival documentarian, offering observations and opinions that would spice up a post-concert oral history published by Billboard. It was no surprise that the financial aspects of the Monterey Pop Festival were never far from his thoughts. "The promoters gave us aeroplane tickets and they put us up in a very good hotel and they fed us very well. But we played for free. Everybody played for free."

While Miller's mind always seemed focused on the bottom line, he was also keenly aware of the festival's mythical nature. In the Billboard commentary, he noted that "Otis Redding was the best thing about the festival" and described Ravi Shankar's three-hour concert appearance as "beautiful". Additionally, he was not above waxing poetic about the impact the Monterey International Pop Festival was having on the world and perception: "At that point, San Francisco was almost the centre of the universe. It was a swirling vortex of energy, and the world seemed to look to it for inspiration."

The ever-gregarious Miller was sociable around the festival grounds, hanging out with the myriad of San Francisco musicians he was already quite friendly with. On the last day of the festival, he found himself backstage with one of the headliners, Jimi Hendrix and his band The Experience. The readily observant Miller found much to dissect in Hendrix, as he recalled in Billboard and Don'sTunes.com.

"I was with Jimi just before he went on stage. You could tell that he was really high on acid and acting real distraught. When I first saw him, he looked like Eartha Kitt (singer/actress) with a guitar. I thought, 'This is really far out. Who is this guy?' Then I went out and watched his set and was knocked out. It was so cool. He brought all those blues and R&B traditions to the stage. He was so far ahead of everybody. So free. So fluid. So much fun."

Miller's enthusiasm for Hendrix would ultimately be tarnished when he found a major bone to pick with the conclusion of Hendrix's set. He was upfront about it when he spoke to Society Of Rock and The Washington Post. "I thought what he did at the end of his set was pathetic. When I saw Jimi suddenly stop playing the music he was playing, get down on his knees, pull out a can of lighter fluid, spray it on his guitar and light it on fire, I went 'Boy! This fucking sucks!'"

Hendrix rubbing the traditionalist in Miller the wrong way would be the only blemish in what would be an eye-opening look to the future. The success of the Monterey International Pop Festival served as a signpost for the future of rock music and large outdoor festivals, a style of event that would soon be made iconic by the arrival of Woodstock.

Miller, in Billboard, could see the future. "Monterey was the beginning of the idea of the big concert. It gave you a feel of what the future was going to be."

He Loves Chuck...
He Loves Chuck Not

It didn't take long for the future to look bright for The Steve Miller Blues Band. Ten days after the curtain came down on the Monterey International Pop Festival, Miller received an offer from The Fillmore promotor Bill Graham. On TickTock.com, Miller recalled the conversation that would be etched in his memory forever.

"Bill Graham came to me and said, 'Steve, you know you're the only guy. We want your band to back up Chuck Berry on his Fillmore show." And I said 'Oh God!'."

And with good reason! Chuck Berry had been a musical guiding light for Miller since 1956. From the moment he picked up a guitar and played in his first group, the music of Chuck Berry had been in Steve Miller's universe as an unending influence. Given all that, it would come as a surprise that when Graham made the offer, Miller agreed to it on one condition. Over the years, Berry had long had the reputation of hiring nameless backing bands in every tour stop, polished groups who knew every Chuck Berry song like the back of their hand. Consequently, no pre-show rehearsals were necessary. All Berry had to do was show up at show time and the band would know what to do.

But Miller was having none of that, as he explained in an interview with The Tennessean. "I said I will do it if he will rehearse with me. I didn't want him to just show up."

Enough people most likely whispered in his ear that a Live At The Fillmore disc might resuscitate what many perceived as a flagging career and, when a deal was subsequently struck with Mercury Records, Berry was more inclined to agree to Miller's request and came out to San Francisco for two days of intense rehearsal prior to the show. Miller recalled in The Tennessean that the rehearsals went particularly well. "We rehearsed every one of his songs just the way he wanted them to be. Everybody thought that they sounded so good that the idea of a live album, pulled from four sets recorded the night of the show, had gotten people really excited."

And they remained that way until the night of the show. Things would take an uneasy turn when Berry had a private meeting with some Mercury Records reps and came out just before the show started. Everybody held their collective breaths. Miller recalled that night in surreal weird terms. "Everything seemed to be moving in slow motion. So we went out to do the first show. We ended up doing four sets and I remember watching Chuck play and he was doing some really great stuff."

Chuck Berry: Live At The Fillmore was a reasonable success upon release and would prove to be a particularly satisfying outing for Miller. Critics inevitably praised its rock and blues moments and would indicate that a lot of the album's fire power was due in no small measure to the presence of Miller and his band. The chemistry between Berry and Miller had proved to be so good that the Steve Miller Blues Band would be called upon to back Berry on an estimated forty shows over the next couple of years.

Shows that would inevitably try Miller's patience. It seemed that Berry would use the occasion of Miller being back in the fold to lapse into a myriad of issues. Berry would often fly to cross-country gigs at the last possible moment, frequently arriving just in time or even later, a situation that, to perfectionist Miller, made everything crucially challenging. This often resulted in Miller and his band having to improvise an unexpected set until Berry arrived. There would also be those shows when Berry who, at least mentally, had a forty-five-minute performance limit, after which he would just walk off the stage. In one instance, a promoter who begged him to come back out and do an encore, was told by Berry that he would do an encore for an extra thousand-dollar payment.

Miller told The Tennessean how bad things could get around Berry, and about the night when he decided he'd finally had enough. "We did a lot of shows like this and it eventually got to where he was kind of cranky with the band. He'd stop everything in the middle of a show and it got to be a problem. One night he embarrassed the band on stage. I walked off the stage and said, 'If you ever fucking do that to me again, Chuck, you can fucking get your own band and your own equipment and start carrying your own amp. Because I'm not ever going on stage with you again if that happens.' Once I had that showdown with him backstage, from that time on, he was just great."

"And it never happened again."

What They Were Expecting Were Dummies

The Monterey International Pop Festival was a success on any number of levels. Great bands and musicians got together to make great music. Critically it was a success. Financially it made a profit and there would be a very good documentary film to boot. So far, everything connected to this get-together in front of an audience of thousands was solid. But there would be more to the aftermath of Monterey Pop.

Shortly after Monterey Pop, guitarist Curly Cooke became very sick. The band attempted to soldier on with Cooke but, as Cooke recalled in RockProsography101.com, "I was so sick that I had a hard time playing. I was so sick that I was seeing stars on stage."

Cooke eventually ended up in the hospital and subsequently left the band. Miller and company attempted to carry on as a four-piece but, to Miller's way of thinking, there was a need for a second guitarist.

Around that time, an old friend and long-ago bandmate, Boz Scaggs, reappeared. After a period of time in Sweden, in which he released a solo album on Polydor that did not do well, Scaggs, reportedly owing to a change in his US draft status, was now free and clear and, shortly thereafter, reconnected with Miller and was invited to join The Steve Miller Blues Band. Scaggs recalled how it all came about on Beautifulboz.com. "I was living in Stockholm at the time and I received a postcard from Steve, asking me if I would be interested in coming back to the States and filling in a spot in the band. I said 'yeah I was kind of interested' and they sent me a plane ticket and I went back and tried it out and I stayed."

Scaggs did so reluctantly. He was still heavily the soul and blues cat and did not really get the whole psychedelic rock/freak-out scene. But Miller made a strong case for how cool everything would be, and Scaggs was, one more time, a member in good standing in Steve Miller's universe.

Meanwhile, the record company shark hunt was continuing.

Record company executives in suits smelled dollar signs in this new age of new music and ushered in a new age of the wild, wild west. The festival would ultimately launch the careers of many of the groups and musicians. Careers were literally forged on the heels of Monterey Pop. Within a year, most of the big San Francisco bands had lucrative record deals.

One of these bands was The Steve Miller Blues Band, which proved particularly difficult to secure. Miller, who would wax sarcastic about the situation, revealed in Rolling Stone that in the ten months following Monterey Pop, the band entertained record label offers from no less than thirteen labels, with executives seeming indifferent.

"The record companies, typically, did not understand anything about music. They were given instructions to go after one of the four most popular San Francisco groups at the festival. It didn't really matter which one. All they wanted was to sign the phenomena."

By this time, Miller was pretty hip and justifiably cynical about those courting his services, as he would reflect in Guitar Player. "Record labels weren't interested in dealing with educated people. What they were expecting was that musicians were dummies."

What they had not anticipated was that Miller had already immersed himself in the business side of music for what seemed like eons. He observed as fellow Bay Area groups signed what he deemed to be less than lucrative deals. Over nearly a year, he fielded numerous offers but walked away empty-handed. Capitol Records remained persistent in courting Miller, known for getting the best of contracts while leaving bands with little to show for it. It was at this juncture that Miller enlisted the help of Harvey Kornspan, a life explorer, scene devotee, and most recently, Miller's manager, who provided additional context in an interview with DiggerDocs.com.

"Miller was in Berkeley. I went to see him a few times and we talked. I wanted to get into the entertainment thing, and I did. I started to manage him. I started to invest a lot of time in the Miller band. I used to do things like get airline tickets for the band. We played a lot. We were part of a group of bands that was playing all the time. It became a viable business."

And so, when negotiations with Capitol were reaching a critical juncture, it seemed only natural for Kornspan to step in and do the heavy lifting. How he managed the negotiations was anybody's guess, but Capitol ultimately said yes to one of the most lucrative contracts in rock and roll history. It was broken down in dollars and cents in GuitarPlayer.com and PeelFandom.com. Steve Miller would receive a fifty-thousand dollar advance, a ten-thousand bonus for one year, four one-year options totalling seven-hundred-and-fifty-thousand dollars, twenty-five-thousand dollars in promotion money, a thirty-two-cent royalty on each album sold for a total of eight-hundred-and-sixty-thousand dollars over five years. But perhaps the most gratifying to Miller was that he would receive complete artistic control over his work.

Word of The Steve Miller Blues Band signing was lighting in the press. Many pundits were saying that it was the second-largest of Capitol Records' signings after The Beatles. True or press hyperbole, nobody could argue that Miller and company had made out like a bandit.

After the requisite welcome and gladhanding, Miller was anxious to get down to the business of getting in the studio and making music, as he excitedly put it in SteveMillerBand.com. "I was really excited to begin recording. I had written a bunch of songs and was ready to go."

However, Miller soon fell prey to Capitol Records' agendas and politics. For openers in the all-important engineering cadre, as Miller remembered, "were crew-cut, country types who made no bones about the fact that they didn't like hippies. I wasn't getting any help from anybody at Capitol. We were being moved back and forth between studios at odd hours, usually beginning at midnight and sometimes we'd have to change studios in the middle of the night because another musician had already booked that studio. At one point all the engineers just walked out of a session."

Miller was growing more agitated and unhappy by the day. Finally, one morning at 3:30, he couldn't take it anymore and, as he said in SteveMillerBand.com, he got on the phone and exploded. "I called up my producer, John Palladino, in the middle of the night and I said 'I'll be right over. You can have your contract back. You can have the money back. You can have it all back.' The producer started freaking out, yelling 'no no no'."

"Then we started trying to figure out where we were going to record."

Abracadabra

Wild In The UK

Steve Miller appeared to have Capitol Records over a barrel. The notion that the label had potentially made its most significant signing since The Beatles, only to push the artist to the brink of wanting out of his contract due to the pettiness of the label's vaunted engineering department, was not a path Capitol Records wished to go down. Therefore, in the days surrounding Miller's meltdown, the label bent over backwards to appease him.

The situation led the label to send The Steve Miller Blues Band to the famed Olympic Studios in London for the production of their first album, initially under the guidance of none other than the Beatles' legendary George Martin. However, Martin was called away at the last minute to assist The Beatles with fine-tuning Sgt. Pepper's Lonely Hearts Club Band and Magical Mystery Tour. A suitable replacement was found in the form of the highly regarded engineer Glyn Johns, known for his work with Chris Farlowe, The Small Faces, and The Rolling Stones. The Steve Miller Blues Band's album became his inaugural project as a producer.

Before the band travelled to England, Miller and the group met with Johns to gauge each other's direction for what would become the album Children Of The Future. The tone of those meetings made it clear to band member Jim Peterman, as recounted in TheStrangeBrew.com, that while the conversations were pleasant enough on the surface, there was an underlying reality, particularly as conveyed by Miller, as to who would be leading the production. "Glyn was very much the rock star. He was very easy going and very casual. We talked about the project at length. We didn't want someone to come in and make the album the way they thought it should sound. We wanted to make sure that we were the ones keeping the reins."

And so the parameters of making Children Of The Future were quickly set. Miller would act as defacto producer while Johns would work as engineer. The album would be recorded over a six-week schedule between January and March 1968. Everything and everybody seemed in sync and on board as the band made a five-day voyage on the SS United States (which would allow for two practice gigs on board to iron out any technicalities).

The session was shaping up as one big love fest. But by the time the group and their extended entourage settled in and began their first days in Olympic Studios, tensions, in particular between Miller and Johns began to smoulder in what was shaping up to be an enticing mixture of psychedelic rock and blues. It was a daring musical mixture going in, and one that did not take long to cause friction on both sides of the studio board.

Miller, in a SteveMillerBand.com interview recalled the butting of heads with Johns. "Glyn and I had lots of arguments. He was ambitious and was very good at what he did. But we pretty much had to keep him off the record. We had to keep him from playing bass, the tambourine. Glyn was all about making the sound bigger. I argued with him all the time."

Glyn saw things differently.

With Miller as producer, four weeks went by with a lot of experimentation going on but absolutely no music was being created. A keen observer, Johns could sense a growing discontent by the rest of the musicians in the fact that nothing was being accomplished and that the clock was definitely ticking with nothing concrete to show for it.

It was time for a come-to-Jesus moment between Miller and Johns, as he recalled in his memoir Sound Man: A Life In Music and excerpted in BluesHighway.com. "Steve was the producer and he was supposed to be producing. We had six weeks to make the record and after four weeks the band had not achieved anything. They were just dicking around. Steve had spent the entire time experimenting with different ideas for songs, arrangements and recording techniques. I got really bored so I said to Steve, 'Sorry mate, but I can't do this anymore. You're wasting my time and everybody else's time. You're never going to make a record like this. I'm off.' Steve panicked a bit and said, 'What can we do?'. I said, 'you need somebody to produce you.' He said, 'would you do it?'. I said 'yeah' and so I got the producing job on the spot."

With Glyn Johns at the helm, Children Of The Future was completed in two weeks. But not before various members of The Steve Miller Blues Band entourage and, at one point, several members of the band were arrested by London bobbies — on the dual charge of trafficking in drugs and possessing a firearm.

As Glyn explained in his book Sound Man: A Life In Music, "It seems a friend from San Francisco had sent a pillow containing a fruitcake, which (reportedly) contained some drugs to London and to manager Harvey Kornspan. The postal service was suspicious and had their drug-sniffing dog go through the package. The dog had a positive reaction and the band was busted."

With the gun charge thrown in (which was, in actuality, an unusable flare gun found in the residence where the band and their entourage were staying), The Steve Miller Blues Band (minus Miller and Scaggs, who happened to be elsewhere when the arrests were made) found themselves soon on their way to jail. Frantic wives and girlfriends were on the phone to the one person they felt could get them out of this mess: newly minted producer Glyn Johns, who recounted what happened next in his book.

"One evening I got a frantic phone call from (band member) Jim Peterman's wife. She said all of them had been arrested, were in jail and were to appear in court the following morning charged with transporting drugs and with possession of a firearm. She was frantic and wanted to know if I could present myself in court the next morning to guarantee everybody's good character and post bail until their manager worked the messy business out with the courts."

Johns was always an accommodating sort, but he admitted in his book that he was rather reluctant to step in and assist his American charges, especially considering he was nearing the completion of his first album as a producer. "He didn't really like the idea of associating with these people under the circumstances, and suppose this got in the press. So I showed up in court the next morning in my best suit and sporting my best accent. That did the trick. Both charges, after some tense moments, were dismissed with a twenty-five-dollar fine for each member and a year's probation on narcotics charges."

That would not be the last word on the matter, as Jim Peterman recalled in TheStrangeBrew.com. "They were finishing up the album and they had some England gigs already booked. After further discussion, we were told that we could finish the album, but they pulled our work visa on the gigs we had already booked. More lawyers stepped in at that point. The result was a hollow victory. We would be deported, but we would be allowed to finish the album."

As chaotic as the Children Of The Future sessions were, Miller had to admit in a Vulture.com conversation that there was much to be learned, musically, once Johns had taken over the production. "We sort of learned the English approach to recording and that got to be a regular part of our regular working system. We would go in and cut a bunch of tracks. We would think about it for a while, and then we would start doing guitar work."

The release of Children Of The Future by The Steve Miller Band in June 1968 marked several significant firsts. It was the band's debut

the
steve
miller
band
uses Sunn amplifiers exclusively

Sunn Musical Equipment Company

amburn industrial park, tualatin, oregon 97062

album, Johns' first production credit, and the first time, as suggested by George Martin to Miller as a means of striking a more populist tone, that they were called The Steve Miller Band. However, it took some time for marketing personnel to adjust to the name change during tours. Meanwhile, Capitol wasted no time in promoting the album, releasing The Steve Miller Band's very first single, 'Sittin' In Circles' b/w 'Roll With It', in April. Despite the effort, the release went relatively unnoticed.

The Steve Miller Band, which would eventually be shortened to just Steve Miller, had barely touched down in the States when they were back on the road, priming the pump with non-stop shows leading up to the release of Children Of The Future in June. Being in a studio state of mind had not dampened the band's live performing attitude and, with a whole album's worth of new material, the shows were exciting and memorable. Steve Miller was in his element.

Upon its release in June, Children Of The Future received largely positive and insightful feedback from the rock world. Miller's songwriting skills and recording techniques, with a nod to Glyn Johns' deft production, were duly recognised. While the album was critically acclaimed, it fell short in terms of commercial success, peaking at number one-hundred-and-thirty-four on the Billboard charts.

If the lack of commercial success and a hit record was a bit disappointing, it would not dissuade Miller from getting back to making music.

Abracadabra

Sailor Makes Hits, Loses Friends

By the time The Steve Miller Band returned to the States and embarked on the tour in support of Children Of The Future, the dye had pretty much been cast. It had fairly rapidly become Steve Miller's band. And at least for a while, the band was willing to go along with it.

But there would be signs of growing tension, as would be remembered years later by then band members Boz Scaggs in beautifulboz.com and Jim Peterman in TheStrangeBrew.com.

In the case of Scaggs, it appeared that the conflict with Miller was equal parts creative and personal. "There was personal disharmony between Steve and myself in the way he wanted to do the band and the way I wanted to do the band. Sometimes in that close a contact we were at odds."

Peterman would be more direct. "It became business and not friends in a band anymore. People were just putting up with Steve. There wasn't much confrontation, but the fun we had with the first album wasn't there for the second. By the time we got to the second album, it was gone."

And it was within the growing sense of dissatisfaction that Miller laid plans for Sailor.

The Haight Ashbury space music/blues concoction of Children Of The Future had been a fairly successful maiden voyage that soon began to morph into a more fluid mixture of pure psychedelic rock and blues, something that seemed to translate into offbeat kind of commercial pop. But when Miller, by August, was already making plans to go back into the studio for the follow-up album, Sailor, nobody was thinking more about having a commercial hit. And that translated into Miller reuniting with Glyn Johns for the particulars.

Johns would recall in the book The Record Producers and Louder.com that Miller, creatively, was all over the place. "Steve wrote to me saying he wanted to make the next album in America. So I went to America and we met up. It was a strange experience. Miller wanted to change the name of the band to Sailor. He wanted to do a concept album ala Sgt. Peppers and he already had some songs ('Song For Our Ancestors', 'Dear Mary' and 'Living In The USA') that would be a part

of that concept. But the idea of the concept never worked out and so I told him to just write a bunch of new songs."

In the days leading up to the sessions at Hollywood CA.'s Wally Heider's Recording Studio, a mental and emotional tug-of-war ensued between Miller and Johns. Miller was meticulous in presenting his ideas of the songs' themes and how they should be played out musically and vocally, which put Johns in a creative dilemma. While he understood Miller's vision, he tactfully presented other ideas that might work for him and for the album. "My job was to help Steve get whatever he wanted, within reason," he said in his book.

The Sailor sessions, recorded in two one-week sessions at Wally Heider Studios, were seemingly operating on separate creative planes. Miller and Johns would meet to bounce musical ideas and Miller's desires with Johns working to iron out any technical aspects of the project.

The producer also knew that the key to Sailor's success would heavily rely on satisfying the other members of the band who, increasingly, were feeling neglected. Through a truly democratic process, the remainder of the band would record the musical portions of the songs 'My Lady', 'Dear May' and 'Dime A Dance Romance' without Miller being in the room. Peterman, in The Strange Brew. com (164) was candid in explaining how and why working without Miller's presence worked.

"There was some time when the band was recording without Steve in the room because we felt stronger without him being there. His being there would have changed our songs because of him always wanting to direct things. We were having fun, just the four of us. Steve would come in and add his parts later."

Through the tensions weaving in and out of the compressed recording schedule, Sailor, in hindsight, may well have turned out to be Steve Miller's best album. There was a solid nod to psychedelia with a Pink Floyd-ish tinge. The individual songwriting compositions of other band members were effective and expressive and Miller's take on Johnny 'Guitar' Watson's 'Gangster Of Love' would become an indelible part of Miller's musical and personal identity. But the icing on the cake would turn out to be a personal and commercial 'Living In The USA'. Musical in the sense that radio would play the hell out of the song, and personal... Well, that is how Miller would explain its origins in People Magazine.

"I came out of a radical environment, the civil rights movement and the anti-Vietnam war demonstrations, and then I got involved in the psychedelic revolution. It was all very powerful creatively. 'Living

In The USA' was put together with the idea of playing at the 1968 Democratic National Convention in Chicago. That was the one where the cops beat everybody up. So, it was a political time. It came out and it was kind of a hit. Then it went away."

Sailor was released in October 1968 to primarily positive reviews and obvious references to the fact that Miller's newfound approach to making rock and blues had commercial potential in a radio world that was slowly but surely going FM. Sailor would reach the fairly lofty position of number twenty-four on the Billboard charts, while 'Living In The USA' would crack the singles charts at number ninety-four, with music prognosticators predicting hits galore. Looking back on the album's success in his book, Johns, in an oh-so-English way, was seemingly having the last word on Sailor when he offered, "The whole idea of the concept had been forgotten. The band did not change its name. Sailor may well have been Steve Miller's best album."

But Steve Miller and band were way too busy to savour the moment. Before, during and after the release of Sailor, it was non-stop touring. By late September 1968, the grind had reached critical mass when both Boz Scaggs and Jim Peterman quit the band. The way Scaggs would put it in Beautifulboz.com was that the split between Miller and himself boiled down to creative differences and "was inevitable".

In the case of Peterman, his reason for leaving was much more basic, as he would recall in TheStrangeBrew.com. "I went back to the Midwest. My wife and I had just had a baby and that's where we felt we would be the most comfortable. I got a factory job, which was something I had never done in my life."

Abracadabra

In A Hurry For A Brave New World

Ben Sidran checked all the boxes: he played keyboards, was a fair to middling lyricist, and had previously played in The Ardells alongside Miller during their UW days. When offered the opportunity, he said yes. With that, Sidran unofficially became a member of The Steve Miller Band – with the emphasis on the 'unofficial' status, as the band was in transition midway through 1969, and there were many questions that needed to be asked and answered.

The band's next album would be their first without the original lineup. Miller, through Children Of The Future and Sailor, always seemed to be searching for ways to enhance the obvious. Suddenly reduced to what seemed like a primordial blues lineup, the band faced the question of whether this change would mark a step backward or forward. It was approaching The Steve Miller Band's third album in two years. By this point, Miller's workaholic nature was well known. He wasn't truly content unless he was in the studio or performing on stage. But would his prolific output ultimately lead to a decrease in creativity? There was only one way to find out. After a few shake-down gigs by a band that was now essentially a trio, fans who appreciated the band before it became a commercial success were about to find out. Steve Miller was about to enter a Brave New World.

The first step was to bring in the big guns. Glyn Johns flew from England to the States, where he and Miller spent a month writing an album's worth of songs that would return Miller to his blues and rock roots. The collection was very bluesy, very rock and roll, with inevitable psychedelic undertones, structured to showcase Steve Miller as a rising guitar virtuoso.

Sound Recorders Studio in Hollywood was the starting point for Brave New World in mid-April, and from the beginning, the sessions were characterised by speed and spontaneity. At least, that's how Sidran remembered it in his autobiography, A Life In The Music.

"Steve called to say that he was going back into the studio and he said I should come out to Los Angeles, play keyboards and work on the songs with him. I was met at the airport by Steve's drummer Tim Davis who handed me a joint as soon as we left baggage claim. When we arrived at the studio, Glyn, Steve and bass player Lonnie Turner were already listening to the playback of a song in the control room.

When they finished, Steve saw that I was there and said, 'Let's try it again with a keyboard'."

The month spent creating the nine songs of Brave New World often turned into a fun-loving gathering, complete with a contact high. The musicians vigorously defended the idea that certain songs owed a lot to The Beatles' 'Madonna'. Lyrics emerged from good-natured banter. In one such exchange, Peterman revealed in TheStrangeBrew.com that his lyrical contribution to the trademark Steve Miller tune 'Space Cowboy' ended up funding much of his college education. Embracing the spirit of an album encompassing hard rock, blues, psychedelic, and hook-laden pop, Miller's versatility with the guitar shone through as he effortlessly traversed genres, showcasing his dexterity and confirming his undeniable skill with the instrument.

Brave New World emerged from that month-long woodshedding with all guns blazing. The album's ultimate success was uncertain, but one thing was clear: the material was strong. All that remained was the final mix.

Then, an unexpected phone call for Glyn Johns gradually transformed Miller's perspective, shifting him from a professional musician to a fan.

An Offer Too Good To Refuse

The call to Johns was very British and to-the-point. The Beatles were putting the finishing touches on the Abbey Road album and they needed Johns' help in mixing it. It was an offer that was too good to refuse, especially when they sweetened the deal by offering to cover all out-of-pocket expenses for mixing the Brave New World album. Seeing this as an opportunity to figuratively kill two birds with one stone, Johns approached Miller with the offer of going to London together and mixing Brave New World at Olympic Studios while he was not busy with The Beatles.

Miller could not say yes fast enough. Once in London and once again doing creative business at the legendary Olympic Studios and knowing full well that The Beatles were out and about doing what, for all intents and purposes, would be their final bits of music as The Fab Four, Miller was in a state of euphoria, as he gushed of those early days back in the UK on The Howard Stern Show.

"The Beatles were mixing an album (reportedly Abbey Road) and they needed a couple of extra days, and Glyn just said 'just come over and stay at my house and then we'll just go to their sessions and hang out'. It was an amazing time for me because this was 1969 and they were The Beatles. Glyn took me over to George Harrison's house and George was so great. He opened the front door and said 'Hi Steve. I've listened to all of your stuff. They're such great records. We love what you're doing'."

Miller would subsequently listen to a number of The Beatles' sessions, soaking it all in like a sponge. "John and Paul came in and did their overdubs and they were done. I realised that there were fifty press people outside the studio and that everywhere they went they were under the lens, and I go 'God! How can these guys do this?'"

Miller's time in London also provided him with the truly miraculous opportunity to share a songwriting credit with McCartney on the impromptu creation 'My Dark Hour'. This song was not only a last-minute addition to the Brave New World album, but also released as a single. The complex tale behind it is mentioned in various accounts, including Anthology and the book Many Years From Now by Barry Miles. It all began when a recording session with The Beatles escalated into a loud argument over a proposed business arrangement. While Lennon, Harrison, and Starr were all for it, McCartney was not. Eventually, tensions rose to the point where Lennon, Harrison, and Starr stormed out, leaving McCartney alone in the studio.

"There was this big argument and they all left, leaving me alone in the studio," recalled McCartney. "Steve Miller happened to be around. He said 'Hi, how you doing? Is the studio free?' I said 'Well it looks like it is now.' I told Steve that I had just had a fucking unholy argument with the guys and that I had to do something, trash something to get it out of my system. I asked Steve if I could drum with whatever he was working on."

Miller readily agreed. What was essentially a way for McCartney to let off steam quickly evolved into a full-blown session that ended up producing a legitimate piece of music. "Steve and I stayed up all night and did a track. I played bass, guitar, drums, and sang backup vocals. Steve played and performed all the other instruments."

The result of this spontaneous exercise was 'My Dark Hour', a respectably good piece of music that everyone agreed should be a last-minute addition to Brave New World. While this decision may have caused some business entanglements, there were definite upsides to having a Beatle appear on a Steve Miller song. McCartney solved the problem by refusing to take a composer's credit and using the long-ago established pseudonym of Paul Ramon for his performance credit. However, secrets like this don't remain secret for too long, and Capitol was quick to exploit The Beatles connection by rush-releasing 'My Dark Hour' as a single on 16th June 1969. The ultimate irony was that 'My Dark Hour' failed to chart.

The ease with which Miller would mesh with The Beatles as good music buddies during his days in London was personified by one incident Miller recalled in ThePaulMcCartneyProjects.com. "I was sitting there in the studio and the band's gear was set up for an overdub session. But Ringo and John never showed up. So we all just started screwing around. Paul was there and George came out and jammed a little bit. To be honest, George wasn't much of a jammer. But Paul was."

****

Reality check: Steve Miller will talk your ear off about just about anything — except his personal life. Whether it's about who he might have been dating, engaged to, or any deep, dark secrets, he remains tight-lipped. However, by 1969, people were simply eager to know more.

Miller had indeed married Diana Kallenbach in 1969. However, by the time anyone thought to enquire, the couple had already flamed out and divorced by 1971.

Abracadabra

Brave New World And On And On

If there was a honeymoon afoot for Steve, the world must have missed it because Brave New World was almost immediately released. While the ill-fated single 'My Dark Hour' failed on the charts, the album, despite being less than thirty minutes long, received positive reviews for the degree to which Miller effectively combined old-school blues, pop/rock, and psychedelia into a potent commercial stew. Though many initially perceived Brave New World as a rushed job, the reality was a noble exploration in music. Any doubts that Miller was not playing for keeps would vanish with this album.

But as Miller would find out, there was no rest for the wicked, and being Capitol's fair-haired boy, after initially starting with disdain, suddenly grew to make Miller the subject of 'what have you done for us lately'. And there was much in the way of Capitol's bottom line that indicated Miller had done plenty. According to Goldmine Magazine, Capitol acknowledged that in the past year, Steve Miller had delivered total sales of over four-hundred-thousand records. It was to Miller's advantage that he was touring twenty-four-seven and had developed an ongoing (i.e., profitable) relationship with the rise of FM radio, which continuously played his music. However, not long after the release of Brave New World, Capitol came sniffing around Miller with the idea of cranking out one more album before the end of 1967. Everybody in Miller's circle held their collective breath.

Was Miller about to say that enough was enough? Not necessarily, but there were more evident signs that the chemistry was cracking at the seams. The band members were often found bickering, and a big part of the tension was that Miller was becoming more dictatorial, making it plain that it was his band and that the music would be done his way. While he had occasionally thrown the band a bone, such as a songwriting credit here or some upfront vocals there, few were prone to admit that the band needed a rest.

So, it was a bit of a surprise when Miller agreed to literally knock out Your Saving Grace in time for the Christmas market. Essentially reduced to their power trio format (Miller, Lonnie Turner, and Tim Davis), with a couple of old friends (Ben Sidran and Nicky Hopkins) popping in and out for bits and pieces of support. On first blush, the material seemed a bit light, and so it proved to be a good idea to get the expertise, yet again, of Glyn Johns, to produce and, in this case, to kick things up with a beefier arrangement.

Your Saving Grace was released in November 1969 to faint but ultimately damning praises. The album was considered just okay in many quarters, the type of disc that might have been interesting if it were Miller's second album. However, at this point in the discography, it was dismissed by many listeners as just treading water. It leaned more towards a straightforward blues-rock outing, appearing hellbent on dismissing his experiments with psychedelia and Pink Floyd-style progressive shadings. Instead, it favoured a less adventurous and ultimately less remarkable approach, veering towards commercial pop. Most of the songs were considered sub-par by Miller's exacting standards, but they were mildly entertaining, thanks to Johns' crisp and beefy arrangements. At their most cynical, critics alluded to Your Saving Grace as a rush job aimed at placating Capitol executives' mania for just one more record in 1969.

Your Saving Grace finally charted at number thirty-eight on the Billboard charts, slightly less than the previous album. The reasons behind the album's production and Miller's rationale for it were open to conjecture. What was certain was that Your Saving Grace was largely forgotten by even the most ardent Steve Miller fanatic. Why the record turned out the way it did was anybody's guess, and only Miller was in a position to defend it.

And if you added 1970's quirky little bit of business, Number 5, to the mixture, one could almost double down on the defence. Miller would gladly admit that his quest for pop music commercial stardom was going into overdrive. The songs on Your Saving Grace had a modicum of potential, and it was safe to say that FM radio rotation might well have given the songs a mercy turn in rotation. But ever the perfectionist, Miller wanted more and better, and soon. In a sense, the pressure was on with Number 5. Once again produced by Glyn Johns and featuring the continued session status of Sidran and Hopkins, this would be the original Steve Miller lineup's last hurrah, as Turner was already on his way out and would be replaced by bassist Bobby Winkelman, along with the infusion of some heavy-duty country music session cats.

Following the so-so reception of Your Saving Grace and, truth be known, Number 5, there was a lot at stake critically. Miller may well have been aiming for any and all genres of music that might crack number one on the charts. The result on Number 5 would be a semi-blast to the past, infusing songs with folk, acoustic, country, pop (in several cases seemingly blatantly so), and old-school psychedelia.

Abracadabra

Abracadabra

Blues would hang around the fringes, as would the notions of progressive rock, but the notion of ready-made singles for the radio crowd was becoming more and more on Miller's mind.

Number 5 would be Miller's first vinyl assault in 1970. While positive, albeit challenging reviews were the majority to varying degrees, and the album did top out at a more than respectable number twenty-three on the Billboard charts, that elusive hit which would reach heavy rotation and have the masses singing along with their car radios, remained just out of reach.

But Miller would assuage any perceived disappointment by hitting the road, where he deeply immersed himself in getting out there and having fun. Throughout 1971, Miller played substantial concerts and shared the stage with some of the biggest names in rock and roll. This was largely thanks to the fact that, while FM stations loved instant album staples like 'Living In The USA' and 'Space Cowboy', as well as interpretations of 'Call It Stormy Monday But Tuesday Is Just As Bad' (T-Bone Walker) and 'Mother's Children Have A Hard Time' (Blind Willie Johnson), the newer material was falling on deaf ears. This resulted in relentless touring, constant bickering, and constant complaints about the band not getting that number one hit single and putting out yet another album.

Upon its release in September 1971, the album Rock Love was being called 'Rock Bottom' by the more snarky music critics. Truth be known, there was a lot of blame to go around. Miller's seemingly continued decline over the past year had resulted in a potentially interesting hybrid: one side a live set and the other a series of studio outtakes. Whose idea it was to rush out yet another attempt at a smash hit is anybody's guess. There was blame in several directions. Capitol, pure and simple, wanted more product and more sales. Miller, for his part, wanted that hit. However, with Rock Love, the material was uniformly sub-par and inconsistent. With the band shakeup now in high gear, Bob Winkelman was the only musician back from the previous album, and the band was filled out by faceless sidemen (notable among them was Ross Vallory, who would soon find himself in Journey). Reportedly, Miller gave the project less than his best effort.

Rock Love would continue Miller's creative slide, reaching its peak at number eighty-two on the Billboard charts. For those so inclined, it seemed that Capitol had a bit of foresight regarding the whole Rock Love misadventure, wanting to get one more album out of Miller before the figurative roof caved in.

To say that Miller had grown tired of it all was an understatement. Moments bordering on depression were closer to the truth. By the time Number 5 had come and gone, Miller, bemoaning his lot in the business seven albums in, as reported by USA Today, was not a happy camper. "This was like a last-chance moment for me. I was on my own. I wasn't trying to do what anyone else was doing at that point. I didn't care about hit singles anymore. I just wanted to make a good album."

Which was when a life-preserver named Recall The Beginning: A Journey From Eden brought Miller back from the brink. More or less because Miller was quick to concede that he was going through some tough mental and emotional times, as he confessed in Parade and Record Collector. "I was at the end of my recording contract, and I wasn't hearing anything from my label. I was starting to feel like nothing more than Capitol's cash cow. If this album didn't work out, I thought I might be teaching high school English the next year."

There was a sense of longing for a scene that had seen better days as a reason for choosing Los Angeles as the place to record. But in the same mental breath, Miller chose to go in a completely new direction. He replaced producer Glyn Johns with Ben Sidran, assigned Bruce Botnick as engineer, Nick De Caro as musical arranger, and, with the long-running band lineup just a memory, jumped to recruit seasoned session musicians such as Jesse Davis, Jim Keltner, Gerald Johnson, Roger Allen Clark, and Jack King as Miller's musical backup.

Miller set the stage for Recall The Beginning: A Journey From Eden when he dedicated the album to Mahalia Jackson and Junior Parker, signalling that the music to come would ignore the always-present notion of a hit single in favour of just making good music that meant something to him. What Recall The Beginning: A Journey From Eden would ultimately be was a two-sided adventure into a world that just made good musical sense to Miller. Side one would prove to be a deft mixture of fifties-style blues, pop, and rhythm and blues, incorporating quite effectively the best of the past and present, while the second side proved to be an interesting, exploratory trip into folk rock and psychedelia.

Miller reflected in Record Collector that making the album was an exercise in balancing out the realities of the studio with his state of mind at the time. "Making the album arrived at a very difficult period for me. For a long time I didn't like going there. I remember at one point during the recording that Ben Sidran was slumped over the console muttering, 'When will this ever end'. So if I wasn't hot on it for a while, I blame Ben and not engineer Bruce."

Abracadabra

Call An Ambulance

Recall The Beginning: A Journey From Eden was completed on 29th January 1972. It wouldn't be long before Miller hit the road, something he loved to do but something that, as the tours grew longer and more arduous, could be a drag, as he reflected in USA Today. "I played huge arenas and was constantly exhausted. I remember coming off stage at some coliseum, handing my guitar to a roadie and saying, 'I don't care if I never do this again'."

Despite his complaints, Miller remained a road warrior at the drop of a hat. Literally days after finishing Recall The Beginning: A Journey From Eden, he was, as explored in a Tampa Bay News Weekly article, tired and disgusted as he drove to the airport en route to the start of a short European tour, when he was involved in a car accident.

The particulars of the accident remained vague and without a lot of details. What was known was that Miller survived the accident in good enough shape to still get to the airport and make his flight to Europe and, subsequently, return to the states and the start of the US portion of the tour, all the while playing in pain and, as he explained in 100PlusSongs.com, with good reason. "I fractured a vertebra. I'm dealing with it right now. I've got like three numb little fingers right here and one bad arm over here."

By the time the Steve Miller tour reached March, the pain which had been minor was now excruciating. It was revealed that Miller had actually been playing with a broken neck and, in the ordeal of toughing it out, had also contracted hepatitis. The tour came to a screeching halt just about the time that, despite some generous reviews, Recall The Beginning: The Journey From Eden had the distinction of being the seventh Steve Miller album to go down in commercial flames, reaching a pitiful number one-hundred-and-nine on the Billboard charts.

Miller would retreat to his parents' home in Dallas where he would spend eight months dealing with his health issues, both physical and mental. During that time, the failure of Recall The Beginning: A Journey From Eden only added further damage to an already battered and bruised psyche. Recall The Beginning: A Journey From Eden had been the sixth album of a seven album deal with Capitol. Whatever he came up with next would be the last album of the contract. And then who knew what would happen next?

As he would recall in The Austin Chronicle, his thoughts were decidedly dark. "I had given Capitol album number seven and that was the end of the line. No one at Capitol said 'Hey Steve! Your contract is about to expire. We need to talk.' They weren't even talking to me. I was doing two-hundred-and-fifty shows a year and they weren't spending a penny on me. Every time I'd put out a record they'd sell between two and three-hundred-thousand albums and I didn't have anybody representing me they knew or wanted to talk to. So I said 'Fuck this! I'm just going to go down to Los Angeles and make the record'."

Miller was caught up in the notion that his life-long drive to make wonderful music had passed him by, and that nothing short of a miracle could bring him back from the brink. Midway through 1972, he did not see a miracle on the horizon and felt that maybe a change of scenery, a return to California, might boost his spirits.

For a time, the relative isolation of the Golden State did not help Miller. But all that suddenly changed when a local delivery man began delivering firewood to Miller's home. On one such visit, the delivery man offered that he had brought a tape of his own music and would Miller like to take a listen. Miller agreed and the pair sat down for a leisurely listen. It was good, actually quite better than good. It kicked open an emotional door, and in those moments, all the failure and frustration of Miller's life and career went rushing by and away.

Leaving him to ponder the gift that was his own music. And making the decision to start over again.

The Joker's On You

Midnight. August 1973.

A group of musicians gathered in the basement studio of the Capitol Records Tower in Hollywood. For Steve Miller it was the occasion of old memories coming back. When he was the new kid on the block, a midnight session at the Capitol Records basement studios was where he was shunted off to by engineers who didn't think much of his long hair and hippie ways. Now it would be the first night of a nineteen-night odyssey to personal and professional redemption.

And the renewal would begin after long periods of contemplation and thought in which Miller, a manic completist and deep thinker, would acknowledge in conversation with Vulture.com. "I was in a transition from blues and rock and roll and jazz into something else. I was trying to figure out a way to incorporate all of that into a form of music that you could play on the radio, but that it wasn't so esoteric that no one would listen."

In the process of figuring out this Einstein of a musical equation, Miller, in Vulture.com, came up with the rock and roll equivalent of $E=MC^2$. "You've got to have a really great opening. You've got to have some sort of musical hook. 'The Joker' had that sort of funny opening with the slide guitar. It had a chorus that everybody could sing. It's got the story. It's got the character. If you have all that, the puzzle is finished."

The birth of 'The Joker' had variations on its origin over the years, depending on the patience and time limitations of the person asking the question. What follows is easily one of, if not the most, concise.

Steve Miller and company had been working overtime, laying down tracks to multiple songs literally at the same time when inspiration changed everything and brought 'The Joker' into play. In a wildly detailed conversation with PRS Music.com on how Miller gave birth to 'The Joker'.

"I remember it was late at night and I was at an open air party, sitting on the hood of a Pontiac GTO with my back against the windshield. I had a guitar in my hand and was playing around with a bassline. The lyric 'some people just call me the Space Cowboy' just popped into my head. From there it only took me about an hour to finally come up with the chorus."

However, the realist in Miller knew that 'The Joker', even in its earliest form, was a bit dicey when he began weighing its chances of being an elusive hit single, as he reflected in Guitar Player. "Back then, I never thought 'The Joker' was going to be a hit. But I took the challenge. I said 'Okay, it's got to be a two-and-a-half-minute song, it's got to play on top forty radio and it's got to follow a soul/disco symphony.' I always wanted to make singles. I liked singles."

"When I took it to the band, there wasn't much of a reaction," Miller recalled in PRSMusic.com. "At the time we were cutting rhythm tracks, and this was just one song out of nine that we were recording that day. It was very simple, so no one thought it was a hit song. So, we went ahead and got the basic track down in one take. So, the song you hear is actually the demo."

Miller would be concise in explaining how basic the process actually was in bringing 'The Joker' to life. "I played a six-string acoustic guitar along with Gerald on bass and John on drums. Then I sang lead vocals and second part harmony. The final part was done by playing a slide guitar solo. It took about thirty minutes to do 'The Joker'."

However, Miller would also recall that the creation of 'The Joker' was not as easy as advertised. He told Guitar Player, "That was one of those songs where I wasn't sure what I was writing. It was so different from anything else. It's an odd tone. I didn't know if it was something I really liked when I was working on it."

The remainder of the album would come together in a fairly painless manner, much in keeping with the very pop, very simple and often humorous stew in an uncomplicated very hooky, very pop orientated nine songs. As witness the Miller penned songs 'Sugar Babe', 'Your Cash Ain't Nothin' But Trash' and 'Shu Ba Ba Du Ma Ma Ma Ma', the overall vibe of the album was pretty much, sun, sand and surf, one continuous free and easy feeling. With Miller at the helm, The Joker, was, seven albums on, suddenly a lot of fun again.

But the good feeling would only last so long before reality began to rear its bottom line head in the halls of Capitol Records. Miller told the tale in PRSMusic.com and Super70's.com. "The album was done, but I really didn't have a clue. The Joker album was to be the last of my seven-album deal with Capitol Records and Capitol had not bothered to renew my contract at that point. So I thought that The Joker was to be my last. That's how bright I am. I remember handing the record to the promo department. One of the kids said, 'Hey! That Joker song sounds like a hit.' I just decided that singles were not my gig, not my job. I told the promo people to forget about singles and to see if they could actually get some records ready for sale in the towns I would be performing in. I handed them a list of sixty cities I was set to start playing in that night."

But on his way out the Capitol Records door, he turned and levelled one parting shot at the promo department, as excerpted for posterity in Super70's.com. "If you think there's a single in it, you're the guys that have to go out and make people play it."

"I left Capitol and hit the road. Thinking I was finished." Happily, Capitol finally took the hint. While on the road, Miller was hearing uncharacteristically good news from The Tower. "They sent a copy of 'The Joker' to all the FM underground radio stations and within three months, the song had gone viral. A couple of months later, we had a number one hit on AM radio on our hands. 'The Joker' ended up being played twice an hour and twenty-four hours a day for over a year on every major station in America."

Miller was ecstatic as his current tour approached its end, and the stream of good news continued. 'The Joker' had become an international hit, soaring into the top ten in numerous countries. Miller had struck gold with 'The Joker,' and his practical side was fully committed to avoiding the fate of a one-hit wonder. His immediate priority was to secure a substantial payout from Capitol, sign a lucrative new contract with increased royalty payments, and, most importantly, gain complete control of the masters. Additionally, he intended to use the funds to make a down payment on a new house in a remote location. However, the ultimate step towards a new creative chapter involved informing the individual responsible for booking his gruelling tours that he would be stepping off the road for the foreseeable future.

'The Joker' had made Steve Miller one happy rock and roller.

"It was really a great time for me. The Joker was the first album I'd ever produced by myself. Even better, it was my first number one single, my first number one album and my first platinum album. I felt very encouraged. After eleven years of non-stop touring and recording, I took the rest of the year off to write new songs and start recording my next album Fly Like An Eagle."

With 'The Joker', Steve Miller had written himself out of the ghetto.

Abracadabra

Choices To Make

Steve Miller liked living in Marin County. It was a place that still carried the hippie vibe, the psychedelic vibe, the sixties vibe. It screamed the element of freedom and individuality. If Miller was ripe for a creative change, Marin was where he had to be.

"The home studio was really just a living room," he told Guitar Player. "But it was a good-sounding room with a lot of plate glass windows. I had it enclosed and turned it into a room where I could practice and play music and feel that it was outdoors at the same time."

After experiencing the success of 'The Joker', it was time for Miller to consider the next steps, both from a business and creative standpoint. He reflected on his philosophical stance in outlets such as American Songwriter. "It's not always about huge giant commercial successes. It's also about art."

And running contrary to the way rock and roll usually worked. When a band had a hit, the prevailing attitude was that they would tour until all the steam ran out and then it was a quick race to the studio to get another album out and then, repeat, tour, record, tour before interest flagged; in the immortal words of pop music, it would be on to the next big thing. Miller was better suited to being the next big thing by virtue of having gone through this for a while, and by taking the advice of a 'heavy' friend named McCartney.

"My goal was to have two albums in the can after The Joker," Miller offered in The Coda Collection. "When I met The Beatles in 1969, Paul McCartney told me the band had forty-five songs complete and in the can which were ready to be released as needed. That sounded like a good idea to me."

Once settled into his Marin home, Miller was meticulous in getting the creative party started. He set up a seemingly primitive eight-track recording studio and set up his core group of musicians in Lonnie Turner (bass), the lone holdover from the early Steve Miller Band days and Gary Millaber on drums. By September 1975, the trio were hard at work laying down rhythm tracks in CBS Studios in San Francisco. Then he took the tapes home, where the real work began.

Miller would recall what was going on in Ultimate Classic Rock.

"That was a period of time when I was working on a lot of songs at the same time for Fly Like An Eagle and Book Of Dreams. I had verses, lyrics and music and I was just interchanging a lot of it until I got everything right. I was totally immersed in what I was doing and I felt like I was really in a groove."

For Miller, the next eighteen months would find him on a creative dervish. He was producing, writing and creating without any outside influence. And unlike previous music, Miller was now seemingly obsessed and, perhaps spoiled, by the success of 'The Joker' and what he perceived as the fine art of creating top forty radio-friendly music. "I had always enjoyed the act of making singles," Miller stated in Parade, "but the more I did it the more I learned. I learned that you needed at least five hooks in a single and the first ten notes in a single have to make people go 'What's that?'."

And it would be one that Miller would emulate. Over the course of eighteen months, Miller would write and record literally dozens of songs ranging in styles from commercial oriented pop ala 'The Joker', blues and more progressive, somewhat psychedelic based rock. He would finally cut the list down to a manageable twenty-four finalists that would judiciously be put across two albums. On the surface, the process sounded pretty complex. But Miller found the whole thing not only logical and manageable, but a good way to get along creatively.

How well Miller's approach to making new and commercial music would work out saw the light of day in May 1976 with the release of the album Fly Like An Eagle. Before the dust settled, that album became an instant classic rock standard that spawned three very commercial and very FM radio savvy hits. Looking back on that album and the breakthrough of hits in 'Fly Like An Eagle', 'Take The Money And Run' and 'Rockin' Me', Miller, with tongue firmly in cheek in The Coda Collection, could only marvel at how the process had worked and how he was now on the road to a whole new career. "I wish I had written enough material for three albums. Because once those albums took off, I knew I would never have that kind of time in my career again."

Fly Like An Eagle

'Fly Like An Eagle' wasn't a creation that occurred one night during the marathon sessions that reshaped the direction of Steve Miller's music.

In fact, to understand the chronology accurately, historians need to trace it back to the late sixties when Miller and Paul McCartney collaborated on a riff – the one that provided the initial spark for a great song during an impromptu jam session, the one that ultimately resulted in an album cut on Brave New World titled 'My Dark Hour'. However, there's more to the song's genesis than just a sudden burst of inspiration from one riff. Its early beginnings predate The Steve Miller Band's encounter with 'The Joker', as Miller would recall in interviews with CBS Morning News and Guitar Player.

"We worked on that song for years. Even at that early point, 'Fly Like An Eagle' seemed to be a song about a lot of things. At various stages it was a song about poverty and people who had been discriminated against. It was a political song about people trying to be creative and free."

Miller acknowledged that where the band was in its infancy had a lot to do with the development of 'Fly Like An Eagle'. "'Fly Like An Eagle' was just a basic funk tune in the beginning. We were a jam band who were on the road all the time and we would play these very long, sometimes as long as five-hour, sets. We were a jam band that could go to all kinds of different places and play anything we wanted, and because of that, the early version of 'Fly Like An Eagle' would sometimes go on for fifteen to twenty minutes or more."

It would be 1973, around the time Miller had decided to switch musical gears, that the song, which had always been hanging around in his plans, began to get serious. "I started developing 'Fly Like An Eagle' and the groove just kept getting better and better," he said in Guitar Player. "I kept working on the lyrics and I got it to where it was beginning to turn into a real song with verses and with a chorus."

As the development of the song commenced in Miller's Bay Area studio, 'Fly Like An Eagle' quickly evolved into a battle of wills between the song and its creator. Miller was heavily into toys at that point, with his Fender Stratocaster plugged into Fender Bassman

Amps and sound-enhancing Echoplexes, along with all manner of progressive keyboards and electronics. These tools were essential to pull together the song's outer-space computer passages, part and parcel of the techno vocabulary thrown around during the days and nights of recordings. The basic sense of time and space that 'Fly Like An Eagle' projected was aspired to by Miller, the perfectionist, who seemed to want it at all costs, as he recalled in Guitar Player.

"We recorded and mixed the song once, spent five or six thousand dollars, and I didn't like it. There was something missing and it just didn't feel like the song the way we played it live. I recorded it again in Los Angeles and then back at Wally Heider Studios in San Francisco, and I still didn't like the way either of those takes came out."

Miller decided to try something a bit different, more in line with his growing interest in organ elements to the existing mix. "I brought in Jochim Young on a Hammond B3 Organ along with Gerald Johnson and Gary Millibar. It was an amazing combination of guys in the studio that day and I got the basic track that sounded and felt the way I wanted."

Miller made no bones about the fact that the 'Fly Like An Eagle' sessions were an exercise in his way or the highway. "I did everything excessively. I'd just sit there and record until I was happy. I did not want to put that song out until I thought it was really right."

'Fly Like An Eagle' was released in the US in December 1976 and rose to number two on the Billboard Singles charts. It would be the first of three commercial singles that would reach top forty status from the Fly Like An Eagle album. But by the end of 1976, Miller would rejoice in what he felt the song 'Fly Like An Eagle' would do for the new phase of his career, as he reflected in Vultue.com.

"'Fly Like An Eagle' was a career-defining song for me. It was a time when I really matured as a writer and started writing much better songs. I was developing my music. Things that I had been working on for a long period of time all came together. It was a combination of electronic music and a really funky groove. I put in some socially conscious lyrics and an inspirational message."

"At least, I hope people think it's inspirational."

Abracadabra

Abracadabra

If You Blinked You Missed This

Between the release of 'The Joker' in 1973 and 'Fly Like An Eagle' in 1976, there was a noticeable gap in the Steve Miller singles discography. In 1974, this gap was briefly filled by an afterthought from Capitol. Called 'Your Cash Ain't Nothin' But Trash', it's one for the completists. The label needed something to ensure FM radio hadn't forgotten Miller's name during his self-imposed creative change of life. 'Your Cash Ain't Nothin' But Trash' offered a crisp, humorous odyssey of the prototypical loser who finds, through several misadventures, that the song title is the absolute truth. The song turned out to be a nifty bit of business, featuring all of Miller's trademarks: crunchy blues rock guitar, clever storytelling in a call-and-response sort of way, and vocal effects to punch up the proceedings. Truth be known, 'Your Cash Ain't Nothin' But Trash' would have made a decent car radio hit.

If Miller had been available to play it live or promote it.

But since he was not, the song was basically cast out to fend for itself. And given that there was no visible means of support from Capitol, the fact that 'Your Cash Ain't Nothin' But Trash' actually made it to number fifty-one on the Billboard charts was a miracle unto itself. Point of fact, Miller would ultimately think so highly of the song that he would go on to include it on the Fly Like An Eagle album.

Abracadabra

Take The Money And Run

When Steve Miller decided to encapsulate his long-entrenched values of rebellion and freedom into 2:50 of classic fifties true crime angst, wrapped up in a pop rock hook-laden bit of radio-friendly business entitled 'Take The Money And Run', he saw it as nothing more than a fun venture. However, he then watched as the song climbed to number eleven on the Billboard charts, and people began lining up to both take credit and delve deep into the meaning behind it all.

Capitol, who initially opposed Miller's inclusion of 'Take The Money And Run' on the Fly Like An Eagle album before relenting to his persistence, was now boasting about the song's success. Critics were delving into unnecessary detail, analysing its intent, dissecting its lyrics, and essentially overanalysing the adventures of Billy Joe and Bobby Sue. In a fit of boredom, they rob and kill a man, prompting the determined detective Billy Mac to pursue them relentlessly. They manage to evade the law and disappear into the night, seemingly never to be seen again. Despite the song's thematic resemblance to 'I Fought The Law' by The Crickets and 'I Fought The Law And The Law Won' by The Bobby Fuller Four from the 1950s and 1960s respectively, Miller went on to discuss the specifics further in Old TimMusic.com and American Songwriter.

"I was always big on the ideas of pursuit, freedom and rebellion. But I primarily wrote the song because of my childhood memories of long road trips my family used to take me on as a child. The lyrics were inspired by a 1950's true crime movie called The Asphalt Jungle, in which two men were on the run from the law and one ultimately betrays the other."

When it came to the nuts and bolts of the matter, Miller said to People that there was really nothing amazingly unexpected in 'Take The Money And Run's' creation. "I usually will be playing guitar or piano or I'll get an idea or I'll kind of find something that's interesting. 'Take The Money And Run' came from a recording session where I was really high-energy. We had a lot of great tracks that were cut that day. We cut three rhythm tracks and I kept changing the chorus and working on it."

Once all the elements were in place, Miller and the band would knock out 'Take The Money And Run' in a day. Once Capitol was talked into putting the song on Fly Like An Eagle, the only creative bone of contention was Miller's decision to lyrically put the phrase 'ho ho ho' at the end of each line in the chorus. Not surprisingly, Miller's decisions were not always popular and the 'ho ho ho's' in 'Take The Money And Run' would be no exception, as he explained in OldTimeMusic.com.

"I had friends who told me the 'ho ho ho's were too corny. I told them that I didn't think so. And I was right because it really worked."

Abracadabra

Rockin' Me Don't Bother Me

The ground rules were simple in 1975. Steve Miller was working and that mental 'Do Not Disturb' sign hanging on his studio door meant serious business.

Anyone familiar with Miller knew that when he was immersed in his work, interruptions were unwelcome. In 1975, he was fully occupied with songwriting, crafting hit singles, and rejuvenating his career, making him uninterested in lucrative tour offers.

Even if the offer was from a superstar band who wanted Steve Miller to open for them at a massive outdoor UK Festival. Unbeknownst to Miller, Pink Floyd were massive fans of his on the strength of his albums Children Of The Future and Sailor. As he described in a Syrus XM interview and Ultimate Classic Rock, the dance began this way: "I didn't know anything about that and one day I got a call from my agent who said 'Pink Floyd wants you to come to England and play with them at an outdoor festival.' I said, 'Well you know, I'm right in the middle of writing right now, I'm working on my own album right now and I don't even have a band at the moment, I can't do it'."

The transatlantic dance would continue: "Pink Floyd's people said, 'Well we really want you to do it'. I said, 'I really can't do it'. Finally I tell them I want a gazillion dollars (which translates into fifty-thousand dollars American) or I can't do it. I was asking for a gazillion dollars so they would go away. And they call right back and said, 'That'll be fine'. I decided, 'Well this would be enough! Yeah I can take a little break and do this!'."

The business side of Steve Miller had gotten the better of him. He got a gig he didn't really want, a gazillion dollars he could always use, and a free trip to London and, well, Miller always liked London. Now all he needed was a band. In short order he recruited Les Dudek, Lonnie Turner Doug (Credence Clearwater Revival drummer) Clifford. "I asked them how they would like an all expenses paid vacation to London to go on the Kenworth Festival opening for Pink Floyd? They came over to the house that afternoon and we rehearsed our set that afternoon. Then we got on the plane."

At that juncture, 'Rockin' Me' emerged, accompanied by a fair share of speculation. One account suggested that the musical component had been finished during Miller's writing spree, while another claimed the song was composed entirely during the flight from the US to London. However, Miller clarified the truth upon their arrival in London, as recounted later in Ultimate Classic Rock. He had a strong intuition about the show, knowing the band would perform just before Pink Floyd. With the sun setting and no stage lights, he anticipated a chilly atmosphere.

"I knew it would be a lousy time. But I thought, 'You know what? I'm going to kick those guys in the butt.' So I went back and wrote the song 'Rockin' Me' with the vibe that it would be played at a festival just to get our set going. 'Rockin' Me' just ripped the joint up and afterwards I thought that maybe we ought to record this one. This might be a good one to put on the record."

Back in the states, Miller did just that.

'Rockin' Me' would be a departure from the typical fare on Fly Like An Eagle. Following the progressive vibe of the album's title track, 'Rockin' Me' initially appears somewhat lightweight, offering a mid-tempo, radio-friendly blend of rock and pop. Melodically, it nods to influences like The Beach Boys, The Eagles, and even includes a subtle reference to Free's 'Alright Now'. However, it's the lyrics of 'Rockin' Me' that truly resonate universally and emotionally, as Miller reflected in Guitar World.

"The song was inspired by my time spent on the road. I was just trying to get into the feeling of what it it's like to be a traveller and having the certain freedom that comes along with that."

At one point, Miller acknowledged in BrainyQuotes.com that 'Rockin' Me' may well be the harbinger of where his music was heading. "Songs like 'Rockin' Me' were actually written to be played in large, one-hundred-thousand-people kind of gatherings and a lot of what came out on Fly Like An Eagle was put together for big, big venues with big light shows."

Book Of Dreams... That's Odd

By 1977, it became evident that Steve Miller had taken Paul McCartney's 1969 suggestion about stockpiling songs for the future to heart. Less than a year after Fly Like An Eagle had effectively established him as the new king of radio-friendly and hip rock, Miller provided evidence that he could surpass this achievement. In May 1977, he released Book Of Dreams, a truly unexpected and remarkable piece of work. In many ways, Book Of Dreams overshadowed Fly Like An Eagle and positioned it as merely an opening act.

Which it almost was.

There had been semi-serious talk among insiders once they'd got a preliminary look at the abundance and quality of what Miller had been producing during his creative exile. Some had suggested that releasing Fly Like An Eagle as a monster two-record set, including every song, would be a good idea. However, from the beginning, Miller's voice weighed heavily against that notion. He insisted that another album would not simply consist of scraps from the sessions. Yet, some short-sighted observers were quick to nitpick that Book Of Dreams was, to a large extent, the same album with a different name. And, to be fair, it did feature much of the same Steve Miller sound.

It was the now-familiar blend of pop and trippy commercial rock. There were the obvious hits in the making, along with a sprinkling of prog/psychedelic elements. Yet, upon closer examination, Book Of Dreams revealed itself as both an exercise in subtle evolution and a refinement of what had quickly become the Steve Miller blueprint.

Miller was always one to experiment with his sound, and he decided to bring in two new guitarists and a group of seasoned session musicians to the existing lineup. This move resulted in a noticeable depth and crispness of sound. Miller was also generous in sharing songwriting credits with band members. However, with Miller once again at the production helm, the result was consistently crisp, clean, and entertaining, regardless of how one perceived it.

Book Of Dreams would immediately prove doubters wrong. The album would hit number two on the Billboard charts almost immediately upon release, and would follow quickly as an international sensation in many countries. Miller, in Ultimate Classic

Guitar, would look at the success of Book Of Dreams as vindication for a job well done. "That was a period where I was working on a lot of songs at the same time."

But ever the pessimist, Miller, in the same UCR interview, was quick to point out the conflict with the good times. "Even when I was selling a lot of records and all that stuff, I was basically arguing with my record company (Capitol) all the time because they were not doing a good job. It was a fight and it was a lot of work and it wasn't a lot of celebrating. On the other end of it, I've had a really creative life, I've worked really hard and I've been successful and have respect."

It's My Song... You Do It

Here's something you don't read about too often. In fact, you never hear about it, not even in your wildest dreams.

A hard-luck singer-songwriter, manipulated every which way by corporate record label sharks, somehow manages to get a particularly angry song into the hands of a reigning superstar. The superstar likes the song and asks if he can play around with it a bit. The song becomes a monster hit, and the superstar generously gives all the royalties from the song to the hard-luck singer-songwriter.

It's a heartwarming conclusion that fuelled the notion that, despite his decades-long reputation as a hard-nosed, no-nonsense businessman, Miller truly had a heart of gold and, at his core, could be an unabashed softie.

The all-too-familiar 'Jet Airliner,' which blasted out of radios all over the world and continued Miller's mid-career commercial run, was a compromise. What listeners got was the trademark pop/rock instrumentals all wrapped up in lyrics that force the listener to think a little bit deeper while humming along to the hit. But where 'Jet Airliner' actually came from, as reported in a myriad of outlets including PowerPop.com, HowGoodItIs.com, UltimateClassicRock.com, and Songfacts.com, tells a classic rock and roll fairy tale.

'Jet Airliner', written by a struggling, blind singer songwriter named Paul Pena in 1973, was a downbeat and angry song about how his record label used corporate fine print to delay the release of his album, Night Train and, to a large extent, crippled what many felt would be a promising career. Pena and that album Night Train and his version of 'Jet Airliner' would languish in limbo until 1975 when a musician named Miller was casting about for one more song to fill out his album, Book Of Dreams. Fate would step in when Ben Sidran, who had produced the album Night Train when he wasn't hanging out and playing in The Steve Miller Band, passed a tape of the album to Miller with the suggestion that he take a listen.

"When Ben brought Night Train to me, I could see that there were easily five or six really great songs on it. At that time, I only needed one song to fill out Book Of Dreams." Miller could sympathise with Pena's plight. "He was comfortable in California and did not want to go to the east coast to record the album, but the label insisted and there would be a lot of contact back and forth. In the end, the label got its way."

"That's what 'Jet Airliner' was all about. It was a very long song and a very angry song. Verse after verse after verse of anger. But I felt there was something I could do with it. So I took the song to Paul and said, 'Can I reshape it? Can I play with it?'. Paul said I could do anything I wanted with it. So I remembered laying out all the lyrics, typing them up on big sheets of paper and laying them all out on my kitchen table, moving the verses around, then I got it all together with the music and said, 'Yeah, I think that works. It's great'."

Miller definitely had hopes of a hit as he tinkered with Pena's version of 'Jet Airliner'. When the song clocked in at a running time of five minutes and forty seconds, Miller reworked and shortened verses, injecting the chorus with an upbeat sense of hopefulness as he whittled the song down to a more radio-friendly three minutes and twenty seconds. But make no mistake, Pena's heart, soul, and musical intent remained abundantly present in Miller's finished product to the extent that a strong case could be made for 'Jet Airliner' being a legitimate collaboration. So much so that Miller decided to give all the royalties from the song to Pena, ensuring the rest of his hard life could have a happier ending.

This collaboration would ultimately see the album Night Train finally getting a proper release some three decades later, helped along by more than three decades of Miller's support. Paul Pena passed away at age fifty-five, and some years later, Miller, in WickedLocal. com, laid a heartfelt wreath on his memory.

"Paul was a very sweet and interesting man who was amazingly resilient and independent. My life with Paul was very limited, a couple of meetings, some talk and some playing music, like two ships passing in the night. But we remain linked together to this day. I'm very happy that the royalties Paul received during his life were able to help him."

Jungle Love...
Share And Share Alike

By 1977, the consensus was that Steve Miller had reached that critical plateau in which he could do no wrong. The song 'Jungle Love' would, critically, prove otherwise. A good many observers of his career inevitably point to 'Jungle Love' as an inarguable low point. Greg Douglass, a former member of The Steve Miller Band tended to agree in a San Diego Reader interview. "I think calling 'Jungle Love' dumb and overly commercial is more apt." (And Douglass out to know because it was he and the late Steve Miller Band member Lonnie Turner who wrote 'Jungle Love'!)

The song, which many have likened to 'The Joker', was, despite what some people may think, a commercial hit; it peaked at a moderately successful number twenty-two on the Billboard charts. Douglass, however, would prove circumspect about the less-than-stellar chart position. "At the time, I thought that was a bit disappointing. But that song has been very good to me over the years. It helped me buy my house."

Much like many aspects of Steve Miller's creative process, 'Jungle Love' wasn't initially planned (or even intended for him). During a break between gigs, Turner and Douglass crafted the song, originally envisioned as a straightforward, pop-orientated piece for musician Dave Mason. However, as Douglass recounted to The San Diego Reader, the rough demo took an unexpected turn, evolving into what he described as "Dr. Seuss on acid".

Apparently it would be at the Dr. Seuss stage that the demo came into the hands of Miller, who was in the home stretch of completing the final mix down for Book Of Dreams. Upon hearing 'Jungle Love', Miller immediately claimed the song for himself. Miller would remember the moment in Parade. "We were already in the final mixing phase on Book Of Dreams and this was all very last-minute. One of the nice things about being your own producer is that you can get things done quickly,"

With the clock ticking, Miller and the band knocked out 'Jungle Love' in a day, incorporating his by now trademark commercial touches with an upbeat sense of humour. Douglass's assessment of "dumb and overly commercial" was spot on, as was his assessment that it was a hit and that he continues to make a lot of money.

Swingtown... The Last Roundup

The release of the single 'Swingtown' in October 1977 marked the end of the beginning for Steve Miller.

After ten years of recording and struggling in the shadows of semi-stardom, he had finally become a star through an evolution in his music. 'Swingtown' was his sixth commercial hit in a two-year climb, signalling something new and appealing to the masses, setting the stage for the future of his career, which was far from over. However, with the release of 'Swingtown', the big question remained: What would come next?

For Steve Miller pundits and critical observers anticipating his trajectory at the end of the seventies, 'Swingtown' served as a majestic sendoff. Beginning with its driving, almost classical bass and drum movements, the song embodied a common Miller theme: the idea of hope and freedom depicted through an uplifting, hometown tableau. It explored something simple yet profound with magnanimous tones.

In a People interview, Miller reduced the concept of 'Swingtown' to a seemingly emotional level, worthy of tears that might well bring out the best of the now and the hope for the future, all wrapped up into variations on a pop style that Miller had smartly cultivated since 1975. "'Swingtown' is a song about people who have been working so hard and who want to have a romantic evening out on the town and dance while the night is still young."

The simplicity and directness of 'Swingtown' is the song's true saving grace. You could hear it on the radio driving down the road in the middle of the night. You could punch its number in any jukebox in the land. You could be humming it in the silence of the night. 'Swingtown' managed to make it to number seventeen on the Billboard charts. In the hearts and minds of those who will live and die by this song into infinity, it is Steve Miller's true magnum opus.

Dazed Days

True or false? After the release of Book Of Dreams, Steve Miller took what was often described as a lengthy hiatus from both touring and recording. However, when it came to hitting the road, that was only partially true. On 28th May, mere days after the release of Book Of Dreams, The Steve Miller Band appeared third on the bill to The Eagles and Heart at the Oakland Alameda County Coliseum. Between 1977 and 1979, Miller would perform a total of forty concerts — a tentative roll-out compared to the triple-digit touring schedule of years gone by, according to ConcertArchives.com.

A sure sign that Miller had cracked the big time.

Capitol didn't waste much time hinting to Miller that it might be time for more product. However, Miller was still adjusting to his newfound larger profile and was hesitant to rush back into the studio. Despite his reservations, Steve Miller's Greatest Hits 1974-1978 was rushed out in November 1978, branded immediately as greatest hits with an asterisk.

The album, containing 'The Joker' and thirteen legitimate chart hits from Fly Like An Eagle and Book Of Dreams, was essentially a convenient collection of all the songs Steve Miller fans already had, making it the type of release usually dropped for Christmas shoppers. There would be a dribble of blowback directed at Miller, whose business acumen seemed to be the main cause for the release. All that aside, Steve Miller's Greatest Hits 1974-1978 sold fifteen-million copies, the equivalent of fifteen times platinum.

Drummer Gary Mallaber, who had been with Miller for twenty years, long enough to have participated in every song on the Greatest Hits package, offered an assessment of the process in RedBulllMusicAcademy.com. "Steve got his first hit off 'The Joker', which I considered a throwaway song. But after that, the next two albums would be a concise body of work."

Miller's plans for the early eighties were a mystery to many. He wasn't hitting the road much. As indicated by ConcertArchives.com, Miller and his band played only two concerts in 1980 and 1981 combined. The only sign of recording activity during that time was a half-hearted release of the song 'Heart Like A Wheel', which, despite being a previously recorded track, managed to reach a surprising, if tepid, chart position of number twenty-four on the Billboard charts.

The need for a greatest hits album so early in this new chapter of Miller's career sparked speculation that he had quickly become a one-trick pony and might rely on thinly veiled variations of his hits in later life. However, Miller, in conversation with The Washington Post, expressed confidence in his ability to create music that was both creative and successful. "To write another hit you have to be really disciplined but, at the same time, you want to get this great, spontaneous feeling on the record and you know you've got three seconds at the beginning of a song to hook people."

By 1980, Miller was keenly aware of the evolving landscape of music. Disco was fading, punk was struggling, and new genres like new wave, synth pop, glam rock, and resurgent teen pop were taking centre stage. These shifts were driven by revamped radio formats and the rise of MTV and other video outlets. Simultaneously, technological advancements were reshaping music, leading to a more sanitised and less daring sound. This trend was impacting record labels' bottom lines, prompting them to discard older, established bands. Miller recognised that real music created by real people was increasingly becoming a rarity.

He didn't know what to do.

Floundering In A Circle Of Love

For better or worse, Capitol knew what to do.

Just as Greatest Hits 1974-1978 was becoming one of the best-selling albums of all time, the label started chanting their familiar 'more product, another album, another hit' mantra, with Steve Miller squarely in their sights. However, at that time, Miller was preoccupied with designing a studio in his Oregon home rather than churning out another dozen songs. Meanwhile, Gary Mallaber, who was in Los Angeles setting up his own recording studio, remained someone Miller trusted to be straightforward. Consequently, in an interview with RedBullMusicAcademy.com, Mallaber had little to say on the matter.

"Circle Of Love was more of a contractual obligation with Capitol than anything else. It was just something for Steve to hand in as an album. I didn't think it had the writing or compositional prowess and power as his other stuff had."

In the same interview, Rick Fisher, engineer for Circle Of Love, would echo Mallaber's impression of recording sessions that lacked focus. "When Steve made his previous two albums he knew what he wanted. My observation on Circle Of Love is that he was searching for something a bit on this one. He would get the band together for a week to cut some grooves and then disappear for six months. Six months later he calls the studio up to do more sessions. I can't tell you what he was thinking or how he was trying to react."

To a large extent, Circle Of Love would reflect the indifference. Five songs of lyrically simple pop and rock, such as 'Get A Home', 'Baby Wanna Dance', and 'Circle Of Love', while not truly terrible, were light years removed from anything approaching commercial success. However, all of side two featured an eighteen-minute, unexpected, left-field, and total experiment called 'Macho City', which would turn out to be the song that keeps on giving on Circle Of Love.

'Macho City' encompasses every element that was coming of age in the early 80s: trance music, funk, something totally weird and out there, and dub. At the centre of it all was Miller, acting as a hip ringmaster, demonstrating that he could adapt to the changing times, as Rick Fisher related in Red Bull Music Academy (230). "The whole rap thing was beginning to happen live and the dance clubs were beginning to take over and make the music and songs extra long."

Overall, Circle Of Love was an erratic collection, flawed but never anything less than interesting. The only true complainers against the album were Capitol, who were upset that it did not produce a hit single.

Reviews were mixed, but by the time the dust settled, Circle Of Love, blemishes aside, sold in excess of five-hundred-thousand albums (reaching number twenty-six on the Billboard charts) and went gold. Capitol had to bite their tongue.

Miller would have the last laugh.

For the time being.

Abracadabra

Abracadabra...
The End Of An Era

The best Miller could muster with Circle Of Love had been a moderate success and, emotionally, a moral victory. But in his quiet, contemplative moments, he knew the reality. Having accumulated hit records, literally thousands of tour dates, and more money than any superstar could handle in a lifetime, materially, he had it all. Creatively, however, he knew he was on the downward slide of a career that would ultimately be measured by the number of commercial top forty hits.

The abject failure of Circle Of Love appeared to be the final nail in the career of Steve Miller, as he reflected in The Word. "Now we were considered a dinosaur band. It seemed at the time that our run was over. The group was only drawing a few thousand people."

That Miller had cultivated an insightful and perfectly logical philosophy about the consequence of commercial success would not be surprising. He had figured out the process backwards and forwards, as he explained in BestClassicBands.com. "There were a lot of artists that were kind of snide about wanting to make commercial records. But the way it worked was that you wrote something. It was played on the radio and then you didn't have to play in small nightclubs anymore. You would actually go and do shows. You could have a bigger PA and you could have a light show. I had friends who were kind of snooty about making hits, but the truth was they would have given anything if they could have made one."

Miller would not go into classic rock purgatory without a fight. He returned to isolation, the very approach that had resulted in his biggest hits, and came up with the germ of an idea called 'Abracadacra'. However, the perfectionist in Miller quickly brought the music to a standstill, as he related in Guitar Player. "The title 'Abracadabra' began as a different song, but I couldn't make the pieces work. I loved playing the music and I had all the sections down, but I couldn't come up with lyrics that were good enough for the music."

Unsurprisingly given Miller's perfectionist nature, the beginnings of 'Abracadabra' would be a long and winding story. It was during

Miller's post-'greatest hits' period when he sensed change in the air and often tried to make musical sense of it all, as he explored in American Songwriter and Vulture.com. "I had been playing around with the music and lyrics for three years. It started out as an instrumental gypsy blues. I wrote this really bad set of lyrics and spent the next several years recording it. I thought about it and just couldn't get the bad lyrics out of my head. They rhymed terribly and they were just engrained in my brain."

However, inspiration would unexpectedly strike during a skiing outing, as he would explain to The Dallas Morning News. "One day I was out skiing and who do I see on the mountain but Diana Ross (a flashback from the sixties and a shared appearance on the TV show Hullabaloo). I skied down the mountain to have lunch and I started to think what The Supremes would do with this song. I wrote the lyrics to 'Abracadabra' in fifteen minutes."

With so much riding on the need for 'Abracadabra' to be a success, speculation was widespread that Miller would resort to all kinds of gimmicks to get the song radio-ready. However, Miller was quick to point out in Ultimate Classic Rock that he wasn't really doing anything new when it came to recording the song. "I just mixed up vocal harmonies and tracked the length and guitar parts with what was happening with the music at the time."

Miller's matter-of-fact approach to creating 'Abracadabra' was echoed by Gary Mallaber, who co-produced the Abracadabra album and, in an interview with Red Bull Music Academy, offered a succinct summation of just how the recording process worked. "I did a lot of work on the song 'Abracadabra'. Steve was doing this particular guitar rhythm. He would rake his fingers across the strings. I said to Steve that that was a million-dollar rhythm. I thought that if we did that at the right tempo, it was really going to do something."

Caught in the critical backwash of the song 'Abracadabra', the album as a whole would mark a turn in Miller's attitude. Much of the production on the album had been delegated to Mallaber. Out of the ten songs on the completed album, only two were credited to Miller. As for the other eight, well, that's a story unto itself.

During the making of the previous album, Circle Of Love, Millaber, along with co-writers Kenny Lee Lewis and John Massaro, found the time to record a series of demo tapes that went under the band name of Tracker. At one point, Millaber and Lewis took the demos to Miller in hopes that Miller would select at least one song for his album. Instead, Miller decided to take all eight of the songs. To this day, Millaber sheepishly recalled getting eight co-writing credits on

Abracadabra, the two Miller credits being the title track and a song called 'Give It Up'. However, the nine songs on Abracadabra the album would play second fiddle to the much anticipated 'Abracadabra' single.

And it would be up to Miller to nail the song. 'Abracadabra' would serve as the perfect reflection of the new age eighties pop sound, blending in all the traditional Steve Miller elements of guitar, vocals, and harmonies with influences from disco, rap, and other elements that were both old and newly-trendy. If there was a comeback from the decline of Steve Miller's career, 'Abracadabra' was indeed the godsend and saviour that seemingly rescued Miller's creative endeavours. It arrived as a slick hit, with its integrity intact.

Despite this, the corporate heads at Capitol Records took one listen to 'Abracadabra' and dismissed it as a piece of crap. In reality, Steve Miller and Capitol Records never had a smooth relationship, even when Miller's work met their commercial standards. However, this time, as reported on The Howard Stern Show, American Songwriter, and BestClassicBands.com, Miller recalls how a confrontation quickly escalated.

"I put 'Abracadabra' together and took it to Capitol and they hated it. Capitol said they were not getting any phone reaction and radio didn't like it. They said they didn't believe in it, that it was awful and that I was finished."

"I said 'Okay! Fuck you!'."

Miller called his European label, Phonogram, and struck a deal to release 'Abracadabra' in every country except the United States, followed by an international tour with stops in every country but America. The result? 'Abracadabra' immediately soared to number one in every country. Financially, Capitol Records took a hit and attempted to save face by releasing 'Abracadabra' in the United States, where the song became a late bloomer, eventually reaching number one.

June 1982. For Steve Miller it would be the end of his commercial era. But ever the optimist, he was certain that there would be more hits and a lot more Miller blasting out of car radios. He was philosophical in Rolling Stone when he said that 'Abracadabra' was definitely not the end, but a new beginning. "Short songs are what are expected of me. People just want the short tunes. They just want that four-minute fix."

Can You Top This?

Less than two weeks after the success of 'Abracadabra' had officially marked the pinnacle of his commercial success, Steve Miller was back on the road from June to September 1982. To him, it already felt like a drag. Despite the triumph of 'Abracadabra', Miller knew he had transitioned into the classic rock category, where bands relied on their past hits. Sharing stages with acts like The Eagles, Heart, and Foreigner paid the bills, but by the final two shows of a shortened run of nineteen performances over the past year, it had become monotonous. Playing a setlist of greatest hits almost nightly was creatively draining and far from enjoyable.

And the worst part? Steve Miller was bored. He cancelled the rest of his US tour and took a self-imposed break from touring. What this hiatus would mean for Steve Miller's mental state was uncertain. One thing was clear: Miller harboured resentment toward Capitol Records. Their lacklustre response to being pressured into releasing 'Abracadabra' led to minimal promotion for the album. Despite selling over a million copies, the Abracadabra album struggled to get a second single on the radio due to the label's lack of support.

The occasion of Miller's first-ever live album should have been a cause for celebration. Unfortunately, Steve Miller Live! seemed to exude so much half-heartedness and cynicism that, upon initial listen, it was difficult to determine whether it was Capitol or Miller who was more at fault. Recorded at the Pine Knob Amphitheatre in Clarkston, Michigan, on 25th September 1982, for an October 1983 release, Steve Miller Live! came across as a rushed attempt at aiming to keep Miller's name in the spotlight. The sound quality was mediocre at best, and it essentially amounted to another greatest hits collection, comprising ten songs and clocking in at a shade under thirty-nine minutes. Despite barely registering at number one-hundred-and-twenty-five on the Billboard charts, it seemed that nobody was happy with the results.

Want to start an argument? It could be anywhere – a bar, a church pew, even a wrestling match. But I'll warn you: Say that the Steve Miller album Italian X Rays is either the worst or the best album Miller ever conceived, and just watch the fists fly. Because, quite simply, Italian X Rays is both and neither, depending on when one came in on the party.

Anybody who lived and died with Miller up to and including 'The Joker', 'Jet Airliner', and 'Swingtown' would have thought of Miller circa Italian X Rays as a new wave eighties sellout of the first accord. On the other hand, those who embraced the coming of 'Abracadabra' and the synth-heavy, to-the-point-of-too-much-already overuse on Italian X Rays, good chunky guitar-infused pop as a major creative second wave for Miller's career were all in on the new stuff.

The irony is that more time was seemingly spent debating how good or bad Italian X Rays was than actually understanding what it was. Because of his continued experimental nature, the focus was on what Miller could do to top his previous work in 'Abracadabra'.

As it turned out, what he could do is play in a new realm. This was his first digital recording, an approach that often overlapped his expected guitar licks with a wide array of synth-pop and sonic arrangements on most of the songs. Without those embellishments, the songs often walked the tightrope of being ordinary lyrically. Was Italian X Rays finally something calculated, or was Miller attempting to get out of his own way?

It all sounded too high and mighty to Miller, who attempted to bring it all down to earth in conversation with Vulture.com. "It's a great record that's totally underrated. That album was the very beginning of digital recording. We were the first group at Capitol Records to use the digital tape recorder. That was a very experimental kind of album."

Thanks in no small part to the fact that Miller had taken a more generous approach to its creation, songwriting was all over the place and shared by any number of musicians and songwriters. Millaber, by this time, was the working producer on much of Miller's projects, and Italian X Rays was no exception. There was a hell of a lot on the album that was new and unpredictable. So it was not too surprising that the dollars and cents people soon stepped in, wondering where the hit was. Miller felt that the hit was always there; it was just a matter of searching a bit harder.

Italian X Rays was released in November 1984, billed as an amalgamation of rock/new wave and synth-pop. As expected, a number of people were scratching their heads, a sure sign of commercial angst on the part of listeners and programmers. Enough people would get it so that the album would produce two minor hits in 'Shangrala' (number fifty-seven on the US charts) and 'Bongo Bongo' (number eighty-four). The consolation prize of an album that presented itself as thirteen songs, including four instrumentals, and the immediate, long-lasting infamy of being one year removed from a platinum-selling album to selling twenty-six-thousand copies of Italian X Rays, an album that, to this day, has the most ardent Steve Miller fans choosing sides.

Miller could only offer a fairly weak defence in Vulture.com. "It was a very experimental kind of record that came out and just sort of disappeared, but it's got some great songs on it."

As Italian X Rays settled at number one-hundred-and-six on the Billboard album charts, it seemed Miller might have learned a lesson. Moving away from his peak years of 1973 to 1976 had its successes, but experimenting with albums like Abracadabra and Italian X Rays, had been disappointing. By 1986, he felt it was time to return to the style that initially brought him success.

In Living In The 20th Century, Miller returned to his early seventies style, with snappy, pop-friendly lyrics, deliberate guitar runs, and little resemblance to Italian X Rays and Abracadabra apart from the occasional keyboard or techno element. On side one, Miller took charge as producer and songwriter, striking a balance between old and new Miller with a mix of down-to-earth and majestic rock and blues. Side two featured heartfelt renditions of blues classics like Jimmy Reed's 'I Want To Be Loved (But Only By You)', 'Caress Me Baby', 'Ain't That Lovin' You Baby', and Willie Dixon's 'My Babe'. While Living In The 20th Century was solid and respectful, it lacked the standout hit that Miller and Capitol were hoping for.

In the spirit of old-school Miller and with Capitol still hunting for that elusive hit, Miller turned to a bit of a gimmick with a song he believed had commercial potential: 'I Want To Make The World Turn Around' — a socially, politically, and emotionally charged piece. Miller saw it as a possible return to the top forty, but he felt it needed an extra push, as he recalled in People (245). "I went to see Kenny G (saxophone player) in Seattle. I saw him open for The Pointer Sisters and he was amazing. I was in the studio at the time so I called him and said, 'Kenny, can you come over and do a part in my song?'. He came over early, he warmed up. He was a pro. He played that solo and he was done as soon as he did it. He played it with a lot of heart. You just wanted to keep him there all day long and say, 'Listen to this song. What can you do with this one?'"

Living In The 20th Century was released in November 1984, eventually reaching a so-so peak at number sixty-five on the Billboard charts. On a positive note, 'I Want To Make The World Turn Around' resonated with listeners, making its way onto the Rock Album Tracks charts for a total of six weeks. However, there was no successful single to enhance the album's reception.

The disappointment of Living In The 20th Century's lacklustre performance was profound for everyone involved. For Miller, it marked a turning point. He swiftly declared the end of the Steve Miller Band era, opting instead to move forward solely as Steve Miller.

Perhaps fearing a bit of a backlash with the name change, Miller gave Billboard a logical defence of his decision. "It's always pretty much been my band, my music and my vision of what's going on, so I don't feel bad about the band. But at the same time I couldn't have done any of this without all the guys and all those people I've worked with. But there's been a lot of people over the years, so I think this decision probably makes more sense."

Miller's inaugural performance under his own name was as part of an all-star jazz lineup with longtime Steve Miller/Ardells member Ben Sidran, for the album, On The Live Side.

Looking back at the trajectory of Miller's three early eighties albums reveals a period of transition for Miller. Depending on one's expectations, his musical direction ranged from highly experimental (with varying degrees of success) to experiencing some commercial success, albeit not reaching the heights of his seventies heyday. Throughout this period, Miller remained consistently challenging, both to himself and to his fans. The ongoing debate among fans over the merits of Italian X Rays and Living In The 20th Century serves as evidence that Miller was always pushing boundaries and never boring.

Abracadabra

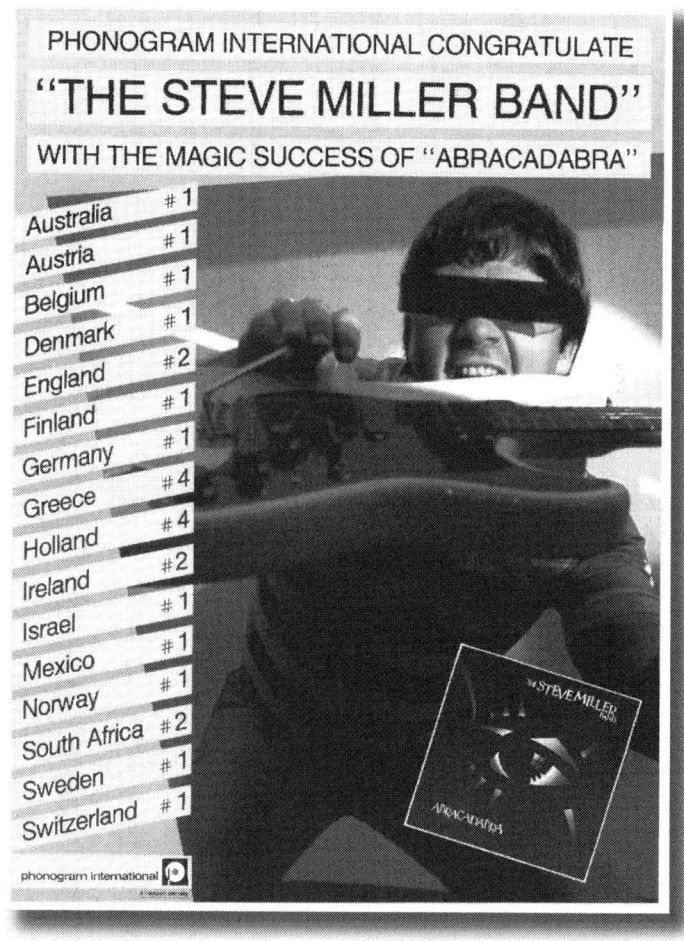

Steve Miller band on KITV

The Steve Miller Band in concert will be featured in a two-hour concert to be broadcast via satellite Saturday beginning at 8 p.m.

The concert, which will also feature April Wine, will be simulcast on 98 Rock on the radio.

The Steve Miller Band live in concert at the Pine Knob Amphitheatre will be telecast from Pine Knob, Michigan. A concert featuring April Wine will be taped on Friday at Cedar Rapids, Iowa for the next day's airing.

The Steve Miller Band currently has the number one single, according to record charts, in "Abra Kadabra." April Wine has a hit recording in "Enough Is Enough" and will be releasing a new single in conjunction with the airing of the show.

All Work And All Play

Steve Miller readily acknowledges that he's a workaholic, fully immersed in his craft whether he's in the studio, on tour, composing music, or engaging in interviews. His dedication to his art knows no bounds. However, even the most devoted individuals need to take breaks, and Miller is no exception.

As early as the late seventies, when his popularity peaked with a string of commercial hits and his rise to major arena rock status, Miller made a radical shift and embraced the life of a small-time farmer in Medford, Oregon. He shared his reasoning behind this decision in a conversation with Amy Hodson on WordPress.com.

"I became much more notorious out there (on the farm) than I would be living in the city surrounded by people. One of the first farmers I met said, 'You're that singer in the valley' and I thought, 'Yeah that's me'. But I'm so glad I did it. It was a really amazing thing to be a farmer, to have ploughed fields and to have planted crops. I was raising beef. I bred some goofy little horses and really had some fun. It was a great experience. It was unreal."

Mentions of his hobbies and obsessions away from music have often been vague over the years, with more attention being given to his day job of rock star. But it appears that a good part of his 'hiatus' from the music business over the years may well have been devoted to other pastimes. Take boating for instance.

Over the years, Miller developed a healthy respect for the sea and viewed the mastery of boats as a valuable emotional outlet. By the early eighties, this hobby provided him with a meaningful escape from the world of music. A notable example of this was his adventure to Alaska, which he recounted with enthusiasm in an article on 40YearItch.com.

"I took a break from 1982 to 1988 and went boating. The idea that you can get on a boat and go to Alaska or anywhere in deep water is some kind of experience. So I started doing it and just never stopped."

During his time away from recording and touring, Miller often merged philanthropy with music. He readily applied his lifelong passion for teaching by serving as a board member for The Department Of Musical Instruments and Jazz At The Lincoln Centre. Additionally, he curated and designed exhibits focusing on blues and jazz. In various capacities, he worked to advance education and inspire the next generation of musicians, as he discussed in interviews with On Wisconsin Magazine and IORR.org.

"What I'm trying to do with these organisations is to inspire a new crop of working musicians. What I'm trying to do is teach how to put a band together, go on the road, entertain an audience and build a career. For me, doing these kinds of things away from what I normally do as a musician is a wonderful opportunity to work with really brilliant musicians and very smart people. At this point in my life, instead of retiring and playing golf, I'm being challenged and I'm enthused about the creativity that is required of me to work in these environments."

Miller has consistently found intriguing pursuits beyond music (despite how one lingering interest he's yet to fully explore is writing his own memoir). Literature has long played a significant role in his life, influencing his songwriting approach. Meeting authors and writers during his travels has only fuelled his desire for the literary world. As he shared in a conversation with Pollstar.com (251), the idea of delving into the literary life has intrigued him for years.

"I always felt that I would end up teaching comparative literature or something that had to do with writing. That's basically what I was interested in until I jumped fulltime out of college and fulltime into music. I've thought about writing my own autobiography over the years and have always saw it as something I would definitely be interested in doing. All I can say is that I would still be interested, and, well, one of these days."

As it would turn out, 'one of these days' would have to be put on hold, as Steve Miller, rounding into 1988, was ready to go back to his day job.

Abracadabra

Abracadabra

Miller Goes It Alone

While Steve Miller was off doing his thing, musically, his output had slowed to a trickle. In fact, if it had not been for 1987's Steve Miller Band Greatest Hits 1976-1986 A Decade Of American Music, a non essential mixture of Miller's commercial hits and selected album cuts released for the international market by Mercury, there would have been nothing new.

Both Miller and Capitol seemed content. Miller was quite comfortable in that classic rock category and reasoned that fans had continued to gobble up older albums to a degree that continued to make him quite comfortable, even with the recent lack of touring. Capitol Records remained financially healthy, largely thanks to Miller's greatest hits, minimising their complaints about the lack of new 'product' and 'hits'.

By 1988, the relationship between Miller and Capitol had deteriorated significantly. Miller often spoke publicly about ignored phone calls and memos, as well as his frustration with Capitol's insistence on radio-friendly material. Adding to the tension was a tabloid report by the Dallas Observer alleging that Capitol had blocked the release of Joker's Choice, a compilation of new and old material, and halted the release of a double live album from The Fillmore. Whether these claims were true or not, the animosity between Miller and Capitol had been simmering during his hiatus and reached a boiling point upon his return to music. In conversation with The Washington Post, Miller directed his ire towards Capitol's executive Gary Gersch, whom he criticised for mishandling a record release. "Gary Gersch was just a gangster, a complete, incompetent lying piece of shit, and you know that I'm just candy-coating it."

The reality was that Miller's ire went much deeper than a personality clash. For Miller, it boiled down to what he wanted to do creatively. Working with Sidran and being among a group of serious, dedicated musicians had whet his appetite for something better then coming away from his time off only to jump back into a grind that he detested, as he remembered in GuitarPlayer.com. "After working with Ben on The Live Side, I decided that I needed to take a more commercial chance. It was better to take a chance and have something new to do than to go back and do 'Jungle Love' one more time. I was getting real tired of making rock and roll albums."

It would be in this state of creative fervour that Miller embarked on a project that was not only a departure from the commercial norm but also a labour of love. He envisioned an album of beloved jazz standards and classics, re-imagined within a modern musical framework, which he titled Born 2 B Blue. Some observers speculated that Miller sensed his longstanding relationship with Capitol Records was nearing its end, and that Born 2 B Blue was his parting statement. Others, less cynical, believed that Miller's dive into the realm of jazz after decades in rock was his way of channelling his frustrations in a positive direction.

Born 2 B Blue, recorded at the Capitol Record Studios in Hollywood, was a milestone for several reasons. It marked Miller's first solo record, deviating from his usual credits with The Steve Miller Band, and it was his first album consisting entirely of covers. The album comprised ten tracks, featuring updated renditions of jazz classics like Billie Holiday's 'God Bless The Child', Ray Charles's 'Mary Ann', Horace Silver's 'Filthy McNasty', and Lionel Hampton's 'Born To Be Blue'. Miller served as the producer for Sidran and his band, including Billy Peterson, Gordy Knudtson, and additional contributions from Milt Jackson, Phil Woods, Bruce Paulson, and Steve Faison, resulting in a leisurely and smooth arrangement spanning forty-two minutes.

It was a noble and uncharacteristic turn for Miller. Would there be a top forty hit on the album? The consensus was no, but who knew? Born 2 B Blue was released in 1988. While there were a handful of standout tracks, reviewers praised Miller's musical twist, and Capitol Records hoped for the best. However, when the dust settled, Born 2 B Blue stood as a clean and polished effort that peaked at number one-hundred-and-eight on the Billboard charts, but didn't reach mass market hit status.

For Steve Miller, it would be the proverbial last straw. Not long after the release of Born 2 B Blue, he would walk away from Capitol Records. He'd had enough of the business side of the music industry. The pressure to create hits and all the other demands of being a recording artist with Capitol Records made it far from enjoyable, as he once expressed in The Aspen Times.

"No one understands how annoying record companies are. It's like with each record you delivered a child and they said 'Oops! I forgot'. You spend a lot more time working on the record company then you do on the record. I wasn't interested in having them come on tour with me and having them tell me what to do. After a certain point, I didn't have to do it, so I didn't."

In hindsight, Miller's consternation with the way Capitol did business had reached boiling point long before then, as he recalled in sheer exasperation in The Oklahoman. "I was at war with these guys (Capitol) all the time because they were always spending money on some goofy band that wasn't going to do anything while I was doing two-hundred shows a year and selling a lot of albums."

Miller explored what he considered the end of the relationship with The Washington Post. "Looking at Capitol's performance over the past twenty-two-year period, I figured they were focused three years out of the twenty-two years I worked for them. The minute they heard Born 2 B Blue (which would ultimately sell two-hundred-thousand albums) they hated it and totally disregarded it. At that point, I realised there was no future for me at Capitol."

Abracadabra

Hit The Road, Steve

Steve Miller had a thing about understatement. He was good at it. 1988, as reported by Songfacts.com, would be a prime example. "I was just bored to tears."

But in Miller's world, 'bored to tears' was subjective, as he chronicled in an interview with Oregonlive.com. "I was on my boat up in Canada. I didn't have a clue what was going on. I had rested a lot. I had built a home. I had put my life together. I had a happy marriage and my life was in good shape. But I was tired of not playing music, so I thought, 'Well, I'll do a few gigs.'"

Miller invested considerable thought into this decision, drawing upon the experiences and motivations that had shaped his life. Music, which had always been at the core of his identity, played a pivotal role in his contemplation. "I had been working seven days a week, non-stop since 1964. I had done thousands of gigs, two-hundred-and-fifty cities a year. It was year after year, work, work, work. We were young and stupid. We played every gig that was offered us. Finally, I had a number one hit with 'Abracadabra'. It was a nice way to go out."

1988. For Miller, it would be a nice way to give it another shot.

Miller would turn to musician Ben Sidran to recruit a band who had worked with him in the past. "Steve had decided to go on the road one last time," Sidran recalled in BenSidran.com. "I put together my band that I always played with and we hit the road. The rest, as they say, is geography."

Initially viewed as a shakedown tour to rekindle his performance skills, it spanned eight shows in November and December 1988. With stops in Pennsylvania, New York, Ohio, Florida, Texas, and Oregon, the sets varied in length, featuring a blend of greatest hits, blues, and rock album cuts. Miller expressed his surprise at the overwhelming response, as reported by Oregonlive.com. "I put the band together and the gigs just instantly sold out. The next thing I know it was time to play big outdoor shows and twenty-thousand people a night were showing up to see me play."

Miller was no stranger to this routine. He had experienced the classic rock arena circuit, sharing the stage with other stars of the seventies and eighties, reliving past memories both for the audience and himself. However, Miller, known for his meticulous control over all aspects of his performances, had calculated his return to the stage down to the very moment and song.

During the years 1990 to 2000, a typical Steve Miller show lasted anywhere from two to two-and-a-half hours. Tours were now scaled down from the two-hundred-and-fifty gigs of previous years to just sixty. Out of the setlist, fifteen songs were dedicated to 'the hits', the ones he had to play. This left approximately nine slots for Miller to have some fun with, and in turn, enlighten and educate his audience. Some nights, it would be rhythm and blues, while on others, it could be a musical tribute to artists like Muddy Waters or Jimmy Reed. Occasionally, it would be a surprise for everyone, including the band.

The change of pace, according to Miller, was one that worked. He told Oregonlive.com, "That became real moderate and easy for me to do."

Miller was now officially part of the classic rock brigade, often sharing the stage with both friends and fellow musicians who had enjoyed their heydays in the sixties and seventies: The Eagles, The Grateful Dead, Tower Of Power, Neal Schon (Journey) and others.

"I wake up every day excited to play," Miller told USA Today. "Each time I hit the road to gig, it still feels like I'm going to summer camp."

Having matured by this point, although Miller may have felt a sense of failure in performing songs past their prime, he recognised the importance of giving his audience what they wanted, as he acknowledged in a Word Press interview.

"It was the strangest thing in the world and it would happen at every show we did. Kids would spend the night on the street in line to buy tickets. That never happened before. It was clear by that time that we had a very young following that wanted to hear the greatest hits. So what we ended up doing was a fourteen-song greatest hits show with nine slots left over, which would be the blues, jazz and some things that the kids were not familiar with. So in the end, everybody was satisfied."

Including, at the end of the day, Miller, who, in The Oklahoman, lapsed into sheepishness at how what he does is examined in such depth. "What we do is play gigs. I've had a great run. It's been an absolute ball."

Miller's Way Or The Highway

When it came to the business side of things, Miller was resolute about his desires and unwilling to compromise. Despite expectations that he'd quickly sign with another label after leaving Capitol, that wasn't the case. Reports suggest that offers and deal memos circulated for a while, but Miller rejected them due to his strict conditions for signing.

"Any deal I made with a record company was that I wanted the highest royalties they'd ever paid any living human being in the world," he said to Betty Lou Music Academy. "I wanted complete artistic control and I didn't want a penny upfront. I'm lucky now. I don't need the money upfront but a lot of bands do. And that's when they end up giving everything up."

Miller was steadfast in what it was going to take for a label to land him, and he was more than willing to do his part, as he said in The Oklahoman. "If I'm going to make a record, I'm going to work on it for a year or a year and a half. It's going to involve a lot of people and it's going to cost a lot of money. It's going to involve a lot of brain tissue."

Polydor Records emerged as a contender. Renowned for its presence in the international pop/rock music scene, by the early nineties, the label was facing financial and corporate challenges, which resorted to them signing numerous acts and releasing albums to maintain stability. While it's uncertain how much Miller knew about Polydor's situation, it's likely the label presented an appealing pitch, leading to Miller becoming their latest signee. Prior to this, Miller was already deep into producing his fifteenth album, the first featuring original music since his departure from Capitol: Wide River.

Wide River, produced by Miller himself, echoed the vibe of Born 2 B Blue, serving as a gentle nod back to the guitar-blues style that had initially propelled him to fame. Clocking in at a robust fifty-three minutes and featuring substantial contributions from fellow musicians and songwriters, the album portrayed Miller in a relaxed state, not overly concerned with commercial appeal. Instead, it projected an image of quiet confidence and self-assurance. Critics ultimately deemed Wide River as mid-tier Steve Miller: quietly commendable but lacking the exhilaration of his earlier albums.

Unfortunately, by that time, what critics had to say was of secondary concern to Miller. The release of Wide River was victim to bad timing, bad advice, and, to Miller, perhaps the worst sin of all, bad distribution. Despite a fairly promising critical reception, with the album's title track reaching number sixty-four on the Billboard singles charts, these factors overshadowed its potential success.

The beginning of the end of the short-lived relationship between Miller and Polydor was marked by a significant setback. As reported by GetReadyToRock.com and The Oklahoman, what was supposed to be a big send-off — a massive tour of Australia — was dead on arrival. "We played my first gig in Australia in front of eighty-thousand people and the label had a total of three-thousand albums available in the entire country. I came to find out that Polydor were pretty dishonest about everything they did. Finally I sat down with the people at Polydor and I just went, 'You know what? Fuck you guys! I'm not doing this anymore.'"

Miller Gives McCartney A Hand

Shortly after parting ways with Polydor Records and returning to life on the road, Steve Miller bumped into Paul McCartney at the Earth Day Concert. Memories rushed between them, back to 1969 at Olympic Studios and the impromptu jam that led to the song 'My Dark Hour'. The bond between the two musicians turned to friendship.

"Steve was easy to get along with," McCartney assessed in a ThePaulMcCartneyProject.com feature. "He's an outstanding guitar player. Very insightful and quick with suggestions that can only make songs better. Just the kind of bloke you want to get to know and hang out with."

Likewise, Miller remembered McCartney fondly. "When we played together in 1969, we really did some interesting work. I don't think Paul had played with very many people. I don't think he had a very broad range of people he was comfortable with. We were really comfortable when we were just kicking out the jams."

The road to a Miller/McCartney reunion began tentatively in 1992 when McCartney started working on the songs 'Calico Skies' and 'Great Day' in McCartney's Sussex home studio. However, a mix of Beatles and solo-related projects delayed the album Flaming Pie for a couple more years. It was then that McCartney's son James listened to 'My Dark Hour' for the first time and proposed to his father that maybe Miller and he should collaborate again. In an interview excerpt from ThePaul Mcartney Project.com, Miller recounted what happened next.

"Linda (McCartney) called up from Bermuda or someplace and said, 'What are you doing?'. I said, 'Just sitting here reading a book. How you been? I haven't talked to you in a while'. She said, 'Paul's working on this album and we'd really like you to sing harmony on it'. I said, 'Come on over. I've got a studio'. They showed up and spent a couple of weeks here."

Paul and Linda arrived at Miller's home in Sun Valley, Idaho, and immediately set to work on the Flaming Pie song 'Young Boy'. The chemistry between the two musicians had not faded with time, as McCartney recalled in ThatEricalper.com. "He's a great singer, guitar player and songwriter. So I thought it would be nice to work with him again. He's a very good musician. He would appreciate what I was doing and I respected his opinion on things."

Miller and McCartney promptly got to work. Miller quickly embraced the idea, as described in ThePauMcCartney Project.com, of being in a genuinely creative, one-on-one environment with McCartney, where ideas and concepts for Flaming Pie flowed freely. "We immediately started listening to the new stuff and to me it sounded great. I pulled out all my Martin guitars, we sat down and he showed me all the new songs, and the next thing I knew I was sitting there strumming on rhythm guitar and singing on a tune with Paul. That was really a special thing."

As noted in the Flaming Pie Archive Collectors Book, Miller would coax McCartney into singing some down and dirty blues on the song 'Texas Blues'. It was part and parcel of how the two musicians had come to a meeting of minds during the recording of the album and, as Miller would acknowledge in Flaming Pie Archive Collectors Book, he would learn another lesson in teamwork at the hands of a legend. "During a session, I got into a perfectionist mode and I said, 'No, let's do that again. I can do it better.' And Paul would say, 'Nah, we're done. That's great.' I said, 'Okay if you like it, that's good enough'."

Following a brief hiatus, the Flaming Pie sessions reconvened at London's Abbey Road Studios. Rock luminaries like the album's co-producer George Martin, Jeff Lynne, and Ringo Starr were in and out of various sessions, adding a series of lifelong memories for Miller.

Ultimately, Flaming Pie, released on 5th May 1997, proved to be both a critical and commercial success for McCartney, who, truth be told, welcomed the chance to distance himself from The Beatles. The album spawned three top forty singles in the UK and topped international charts.

Miller's contribution to Flaming Pie provided many memorable moments, not least of which was his time working with McCartney, learning from one of the legends. This collaboration resulted in a Flaming Pie highlight, 'Young Boy', as Miller recalled in Goldmine Magazine.

"Working with McCartney was really a lot of fun. It was really a neat trip for me. It was completely different than anything that I would normally play or record. He would appreciate what I was doing."

Attitude Adjustment: 1993-2010

Following the release of the 1993 album Wide River, which yielded a very minor chart single but, as Miller described it, was "an international fiasco", he had learned his lesson about his standing in the pop music universe. He realised he was well-off but still on the outside looking in, as he reflected in Aspen Times.com.

The fourteen songs that Miller had written over a four-year period had solidified his place in rock and roll history. They had become oldies, constants on classic rock playlists, providing a financial cushion that seemed everlasting. His touring schedule, depending on where you look for the facts and figures, had been whittled down to a manageable fifty to sixty big-money arena and festival shows by this time, which didn't hurt his wallet.

Miller acknowledged as much when he told CNN.com, "We continued to sell records from our touring and we were in this sort of magical place."

Steve Miller had reached a point where he would never have to work another day in his life if he so desired. However, he had learned from the best, Les Paul, who, at age ninety-two, reminded him of his essence, as Miller reflected in The Oklahoman.

"I met Les Paul years later, years after I had learned at age four-and-a-half to do what I had to do. I went to see Les who, at age ninety-two, was in a club at three in the afternoon, did a two-hour interview a soundcheck and two shows that night. I thought, 'Well if Les can still be doing that at age ninety-two, I think I can do that too'."

Much of Miller's assurance was the result of the ups and downs he had experienced in the rollercoaster ride that was the eighties, as he recalled in The Aspen Times. "When you've played as long as I have, you've developed your own audience. When you've played those tunes in the seventies, kids will discover them, learn them and like them. They hear my songs but they also hear jazz and blues in my live show. It's not just playing fourteen songs over and over again for the money."

It's undeniable that Steve Miller's live show was operating like clockwork, with running times typically ranging from an hour-and-a-half to two hours. While there were variations in the presentation, audiences always left the show enthusiastic and satisfied. Yet, considering the logistics of his touring schedule, it's likely that Miller had some free time on his hands between 1993 and 2010.

And with that free time, there was undoubtedly a creative itch that needed to be scratched.

Abracadabra

The Park Record ■ Section B   Thursday, August 5, 1993 ■ Page B5

STREET BEAT

The Steve Miller Band lit up the ParkWest stage, Tuesday, Aug. 3. The 7,000 plus people in attendance sang along to many of his classic tunes, such as "Jungle Love," "Space Cowboy," and "I Wanna Make the World Turn Around." Former Bad Company lead singer Paul Rogers and ex-Journey lead guitarist Neal Schon kicked off the evening, jamming to many old favorites by Bud Company, and Jimi Hendrix. Rogers and Schon joined Miller on the stage about half-way through the show for a rockin' rendition of "Hoochie Coochie Man," the old Muddy Waters tune. Local favorite and harp-playing extraordinaire Norton Buffalo accompanied The Steve Miller Band throughout the evening.

Steve Miller

Norton Buffalo

Paul Rogers

The Steve Miller Band

Neal Schon

photos by David Bertinelli.

Abracadabra

Bingo! Let Your Hair Down

It's evident that Miller has a short fuse. Historically, it hasn't taken much to set off the mercurial musician. In a conversation with Entertainment Weekly, he drove that point home with understatement: "I don't pussyfoot around. I always speak my mind."

In 1993, it would be Polydor's dropping of the ball on Miller's album River Wide that would send him around the bend, as he related in Entertainment Weekly. "I said, 'I've fucking had it with these clowns. Go ahead and drive it (the album) right into the ground. You guys are finished. I'm not going to give you any of my time'."

During his off-tour periods, Miller was keeping himself occupied, as reported in Entertainment Weekly and Billboard. He had been engrossed in writing new music and, at that time, was in the midst of penning lyrics for a dozen fresh songs. Additionally, he was collaborating with producer/mixer Andy Johns on a DVD titled Live In Chicago when Johns made a whimsical request. "Andy said, 'Before I die I would like to do a blues, guitar-heavy with you, Steve.' The next thing you know I get the current lineup of The Steve Miller Band together over to the Skywalker Ranch Studio and we ended up with twenty-eight songs in the can."

It had been a while since Miller had adopted the moniker 'The Steve Miller Band'. He and Johns would collaborate on the production. However, for those seeking a blend of the new and the old, the album that would later be titled Bingo! featured a lineup of classic blues covers by renowned artists such as B.B. King ('Rock Me Baby'), Earl King ('Come On'), Lowell Folsom ('Tramp'), and Jimmy Reed ('You Got Me Dizzy'), among many others.

For Miller, Bingo! would be a literal blast from his past, as he recalled in Billboard and Entertainment Weekly. "This is a party record, man! It's about getting up and getting ready to dance. It's like the frat party gigs I used to play in college. I went through and picked all my favourite tunes that I really liked. I wanted to make this record forever. This all started out as just a kind of a goof and then it got real serious."

Amidst Miller's enjoyment of making Bingo!, there lingered the ever-present notion of his seemingly perpetual quest for commercial hits. While he admitted in CNN.com that he hadn't abandoned hope of another radio-friendly song, he maintained that there was more historical significance to this album than just a shortcut to the top forty. "This is my pop music. When I was a kid, this is what I was listening to on my car radio. I didn't just go into this to do a cover somebody's record. I wanted to get some material and make it my own, and these songs all lent themselves to that."

As Bingo! was shaping up nicely under Miller's Space Cowboy label, he found himself grappling with the temptation to see it – his first studio album in seventeen years – released under a more established distributorship with a major label. Against his better judgment, he travelled to New York to gauge interest from the major labels. The experience quickly reminded him of why he had initially left the recording industry. "We were in New York, talking to some people at a major record company," he said in Entertainment Weekly, "and these young guys said, 'Man!' This is great! Did Steve write all of these songs?'. I felt like saying, 'Yes I did, and I'd like to play you my new ballad, 'Unchained Melody''."

Miller eventually connected with Loud & Proud/Roadrunner Records, an international label renowned for its expertise in rock, metal, and progressive rock. Signing the deal, Bingo! was slated for release on 15th June 2010. Critically, the album found success, with listeners appreciating its musical depth over commercial appeal. For Miller, this was perfectly fine. In fact, the return to basics, with a focus on raw guitar work, reignited his enthusiasm for music.

"Lots of lead guitar and cool guitar parts have been worked out," he told CNN. "It all just got better and better as we worked on it."

Released as planned, Bingo! was relatively low-key compared to previous albums. It garnered slow but steady attention through word of mouth and subtle yet appreciative critical acclaim. But this was just the beginning. Miller, never one to waste a good opportunity, realised he had enough songs for two albums. Following the old Paul McCartney axiom, he released a second collection titled Let Your Hair Down in the spring of 2011. For Miller, this was all good news, as he assessed in Billboard and CNN. "It's a great group of songs and it gives us a lot of new material to play live. I'm excited about releasing some new music for the audience, for my band and for me to play. The audiences nowadays are really hipper then they were in the nineties when we released our last record. We'd say now were going to do a few new songs and five-thousand people would leave and go get a hot dog until they heard me start the riff for 'The Joker'."

"Now they stick around for the new stuff."

Divorce/Marriage: Steve Miller Style

Steve Miller has always been seen as morally upright. Despite the temptation of the rock and roll lifestyle, there's never been any question about his fidelity within marriage. He's maintained a reputation for being exceptionally faithful.

Extensive scrutiny of tabloids and other sources hasn't turned up any evidence of infidelity or improper relationships since Steve and his second wife Kimberley Smith tied the knot in 1984. It's plausible that Miller's relentless work ethic left little time or desire for extramarital affairs. Yet, considering the history of such behaviour in the rock and roll world, temptation must have been as prevalent as a basic chord progression.

Whether nothing untoward ever occurred or Miller was simply adept at concealing it, those hoping for scandal upon Steve and Kim's separation after nearly three decades of marriage found no evidence of infidelity. What is clear is that the couple legally separated in 2012, and the subsequent years until their final divorce decree were remarkably amicable, devoid of any accusations.

Whilst engaged in the production of Bingo! in 2010, Miller had collaborated with esteemed audio-visual producer and music publisher Janice Ginsberg. According to ValparaisoUniversity.com, theirs was a love-at-first-sight scenario, leading to their marriage in July 2014. The subsequent year, Miller sold his thirty-eight-acre Washington estate, with part of the proceeds allocated to the divorce settlement with Kim.

Like everything connected to the separation from Kim, the divorce featured no animosity, acrimony or a hint of bitterness. Miller and Kim went their separate ways and lived happily ever after. At press time, Miller and Janice are still living happily together.

Abracadabra

An Apple For Professor Miller

❝ Professor Miller will be a great addition to our illustrious facility," enthused Robert Cutietietto, Dean of the University of Southern California's Thornton School of Music in USC News.com (209).

Steve Miller has been called a lot of things, but 'Professor' was not one of them.

At least, not until 2010.

Up until that point, Miller had been involved in various charitable activities, serving on the boards of several prestigious music organisations. He had a particular focus on philanthropy in education and music, notably contributing to an organisation called Kids Rock Free. This group aimed to establish music schools across the country, offering free or low-cost music lessons to children aged seven to seventeen.

However, by 2010, as reported in American Songwriter, The New York Times, and USC News, Miller decided to take his involvement to the next level. He rolled up his sleeves and began teaching practical, face-to-face sessions at the renowned USC Thornton School of Music. He also led Master Classes in Popular Music and Music Industry curriculum.

For Miller, who would make two appearances on campus and in the classroom during the school year, this was serious business, albeit not without a tinge of humour, as he recalled in The Observer. "In my typical class, I would sit down and ask the students how many of them had their own publishing company? They were disappointed because they thought that the class would be taught by this long-haired Jimi Hendrix guy who would play real loud lead guitar."

Miller, in the same article, would remember how their perception of Steve Miller as teacher changed once class was in session. "One assignment to students was to open and start their own publishing company, with approximately four-hundred ideas copyrighted in their publishing company. The entire class would fall asleep while two kids would go ahead and do it. Those two kids who actually did it would ultimately grow up to be the ones who would be running the music business."

The Landed Gentleman

Steve Miller's marriage to Janice Ginsburg in 2014 marked a notably serene phase in his life and career. He transitioned into a lifestyle akin to that of a gentleman of leisure in the rock and roll world, engaging in low-profile activities.

At this juncture, Miller had become a seasoned veteran in the realm of classic rock icons. He willingly embraced the circuit of senior touring legends, maintaining a manageable schedule. This led him to release a handful of low-profile compilation and greatest hits albums and videos through his newly founded company, Sailor Music. Additionally, he struck a renewed distribution deal with Capitol Records, albeit with caution.

As he delved into during an interview with "In The Studio" commemorating the fiftieth anniversary of the release of 'The Joker', Miller found himself in a period of profound reflection and reminiscence. "We've always loved to play music. From the time I was five years old until now, it's always been exciting for me to play. It won't be long now, just another few weeks, and we'll be back on the road and I will be excited and I'll be walking from the bus to the stage to play my music. And to me, that's about as successful a life as I can have."

Miller's wellbeing was significantly bolstered by his wife Janice, whose approach differed from that of his previous spouses. While they had seemed content with the lavish lifestyle accompanying the role of a rock star's wife, Janice was determined to elevate Miller's already successful career into a recognised brand. This proactive approach didn't go unnoticed, catching the attention of Steve Miller Band musician Kenny Lee Lewis. In an interview with Aloadofthis.com, Lewis remarked, "His new wife was really working hard to get his brand out there a bit more, and trying to get Steve to interact with his audience a bit more."

While Miller retained ultimate decision-making authority over business matters, Janice played a significant role in shaping various aspects of his endeavours. From the establishment of his distribution arm, Sailor Music and Silk Stocking Music, to the groundbreaking international publishing deal with Imagen, Janice's influence was palpable. This deal, which expanded Miller's extensive musical catalogue worldwide, excluding North America, garnered considerable attention.

However, it was Janice who conveyed the announcement to The Washington Post in a characteristically understated manner: "We have been working with Imagen for quite some time, and we are pleased to expand our publishing platform into multiple territories."

The significance of having a life and working partner all rolled into one became apparent when Janice intervened to salvage hundreds of songs that Miller had relegated to obscurity. Miller's relentless pursuit of musical perfection had led to over eight-hundred song fragments being stored on tapes and ultimately forgotten about in a warehouse he seldom acknowledged or visited. It was only when Janice started asking about the warehouse filled with tapes and music spanning over forty years that Miller felt compelled to revisit them, as he recounted in Vulture.com.

"I was ready to throw it (the tapes) all out, but my wife convinced me otherwise. She would be like, 'Oh come on. Let's go to the warehouse and listen to the stuff you did forty years ago.' And I would be like, 'Nah'. My thought about it was, 'Look, when I've made an album, I know what I've written and I know what I've done.' When it came time to put out an album, I took the best that I had. If I didn't put something out, I didn't particularly want to go back and listen to it again."

Miller eventually heeded Janice's encouragement to visit the warehouse and listen to the old material. Janice shared her reflections on what Miller discovered when he entered her listening room and began sampling the 800 'rejects' curated by her, as recounted in CantonRep.com.

"I would play him the song 'Crossroads' from 1973 and he really liked it. Then I showed him the tape of the television show Don Kirschner's Rock Concert that he immediately considered one of his favourite performances. So there we were, all of a sudden, sitting there, listening to all these old songs and performances and creating the story with the artist."

A high point for Miller in these exploratory listening sessions would be the song 'Industrial Military Complex Hex', which he would reflect fondly upon with Vulture.com. "I just love it. It was just one of those songs that just sort of came out briefly and then just disappeared. But then we just started jamming on it, it got a lot better. It was simply a matter of recording it too soon. When my wife found the tape with the jamming on it, I went, 'Wow! What is that?'"

She said, "Well, honey, I think that's you."

Miller Makes Peace... Sort Of

Steve Miller embodied the quintessence of a rock and roller: creatively driven, egoistic with a 'my way or the highway' attitude, and astute in the intricacies of the music business. This astuteness became apparent in the mid-2000s when, despite past conflicts with Capitol Records, he reconciled with the label, by then under the ownership of Universal Music Group.

Miller and Capitol had essentially been a non-factor in each other's lives since the musician stopped making pop music in the mid-nineties, which was the label's bread and butter when it came to Miller. Compounded by numerous financial and professional conflicts with the label's executives, it's unsurprising that Miller left Capitol with no desire to engage with them in any capacity in the future.

Until Universal Music Group President Bruce Resnikoff came knocking, figuratively, at Miller's door with an offer to make up for the years of bad blood. Resnikoff, known for his pragmatic approach, understood Miller's perspective. In a Washington Post article, Resnikoff demonstrated his understanding of Miller and what drove him. "Miller was brilliant and had one of the greatest archives of material an artist had ever kept. Is he difficult? I would say that he has a vision, and he has talent, and people with vision and talent can be difficult."

Miller and Resnikoff ultimately agreed to a meeting to address the past issues between the label and the musician. Resnikoff's sincerity in offering a new Capitol deal, powered by Universal, impressed Miller. The proposed deal included providing Miller with his own team of business and financial professionals in exchange for North American rights to Miller's warehouse and vault, containing music and related elements of his career, as well as upcoming greatest hits collections and any new music collections. Miller was ready to sign on the dotted line, but one obstacle remained. Miller, always meticulous about royalties and audits, promptly presented Resnikoff with the latest audit and back royalties owed for a long time. In response, Resnikoff promptly arranged for Universal to issue a cheque for six-hundred-thousand dollars to cover all back royalties. Miller's response was immediate.

"I love these guys."

Abracadabra

The Hits Are Back

Miller, though in love, approached his new signing with UMG/Capitol with caution. While there was no chance of him returning to the pop music of yesteryear, the opportunity arose to revisit his greatest hits in innovative ways.

To kick off the wave of revisiting classic Steve Miller material, the first release was The Joker Live, a clever nod to the fortieth anniversary of the original album's release. Miller, in a press release accompanying The Joker Live, shared how the album originated from live performances during tours in the mid-2000s. Released through his own Sailor label as a direct digital download, it may have been a minor endeavour, but it was certainly clever.

"We were on tour in the mid 2000's when several friends and colleagues reminded me that it was the fortieth birthday of the release of The Joker album. I smiled and started playing the whole album's songs live again and, at the end of the last tour, I realised that we had a great new album for the fans."

Feeling a sense of obligation to his long-supportive fans, Miller swiftly delved back into the archives for Live At The Carousel Ballroom San Francisco 1968. This release, available as another Sailor Music digital download, captured The Steve Miller Band during a significant moment. The album showcased a predominantly blues-oriented set, with only 'Living In The USA' hinting at the commercial success that lay ahead.

By 2017, the dust had settled between Miller and his loosely realigned deal with Capitol/UMG. He felt he was being treated a lot more fairly than he had been. The respect was there and the royalty payments were coming his way in a timely manner. To Miller's way of thinking, he felt that maybe it was time to throw Capitol a bone, on his terms, of course. For him, this didn't entail anything new or overtly radio-friendly. Yet, Miller's creative mind was constantly exploring fresh ways to present his extensive repertoire, honed over many years.

Enter an album including everything but the kitchen sink, titled Ultimate Hits, released in September 2017. Compiled by Miller himself, Ultimate Hits offered an insightful glimpse into what had made him a true creative force. The standard edition featured twenty-two cuts, encapsulating Miller's fifty-plus years in music. Additionally, a deluxe edition included the standard tracks along with the entire Greatest Hits 1974-1978 collection, totalling forty songs. Both editions featured a mix of commercial hits, unreleased studio tracks, and live cuts. Miller expressed humility regarding the enormity of the project in an interview with U Discover Music. "Selecting material to include in these two collections and revisiting the creation of these recordings reminds me of how I've been blessed to work with so many wonderful musicians, engineers and friends over the years."

A Deep Dive Into The Vault

Around the time of the release of Ultimate Hits, Miller hinted at future plans for ambitious super collections. His comments were somewhat vague, leading many to speculate that he might be teasing Capitol Records. After all, Ultimate Hits had already provided a comprehensive look into what made Steve Miller tick. Some questioned how much more there was to uncover.

Two years later, in 2019, Welcome To The Vault provided the answer. This extravaganza featured three CDs and a DVD, boasting fifty-two audio tracks and twenty-one live performances. But it wasn't just another supersized greatest hits collection; it delved deep into Miller's archives. There were studio demos, outtakes, live recordings, five previously unreleased tracks, and more variations of songs that never made it out of the blocks. Welcome To The Vault offered an up-close and personal look at Steve Miller's constant battle with perfection and his creative process. Post-release, much of the press focused on the logistics of alternative tracks, such as the various verses of 'Fly Like An Eagle' showcased on the album. Miller, speaking to BestClassicBand.com, seemed bemused by the interest in his hoarding tendencies when it came to his music.

"I have a warehouse where I keep all of my stuff. It's twenty-thousand square feet and it contains fifty years of showbiz junk and records. If you want something, you go in and it's all indexed. That was part of the project. We just had to clean it all up."

Miller would also acknowledge in Billboard that the content of Welcome To The Vault was a subtle criticism of commercial radio. He felt that commercial radio had been harsh and challenging for him over many years, and the collection was a way to express his feelings about that. "You sort of see in the alternative versions of songs like 'Swingtown' what the limitations of commercial radio can do to a piece of music. I'm glad we're getting the alternative versions of a lot of my songs out there for people to hear."

A big shout-out was deservedly pointed in the direction of Miller's wife Janice, who helped to push her husband away from his perfectionist attitude. Her contribution would be duly noted in conversations with Billboard and Best Classic Bands.com. "It always boiled down to what I didn't want to release and what I did release. And Janice was always like, 'Come on man! You've got to do this!'. I just had this realisation that it wasn't something for me to do. I worked on these records and only wanted the stuff I put out to be perfect."

"Janice found a lot of stuff in the warehouse. I recorded a lot of things that never got released. We (the band) used to go into the studio, set up our equipment and we'd jam for an hour or two and a lot of stuff would get recorded and we wouldn't even think about it. A lot of guitar work wasn't being put on my pop records. I was trying to write rock and roll, so a lot of stuff we were playing just got lost and I forgot about it. Until Janice found things that were really fun."

Over the years, there had been several collections proclaiming to be Miller's greatest this or ultimate that, but it would take Welcome To The Vault to show even his most devoted fans what Steve Miller was: really great and really ultimate.

Them's Fighting Words

8th April 2016.

On the day of his induction into the Rock and Roll Hall of Fame, Steve Miller didn't just accept the honour gracefully — he used it as an opportunity to challenge the institution.

The ceremony began with a heartfelt introduction by members of The Black Keys, setting a warm tone. As Miller took the stage, he was met with continuous applause from the audience. He began to share his biography, following the usual script of such ceremonies.

Until the shit unexpectedly hit the fan.

As reported by The New York Times and countless other assembled media, Miller punctuated the good vibes by taking some unexpected shots at the Rock and Roll Hall of Fame. "I encourage you to keep expanding your vision and to be more inclusive to women, and to do more to support music education in the schools." There was a bit of silence and notable discomfort in the audience as Miller launched into a mini set of 'Fly Like An Eagle', 'Rockin'Me' and 'The Joker' to polite applause before going backstage where the press questioned him on his tirade. Things got heated as Miller continued to fire away at the ceremony and the organisation.

"The whole induction process is unpleasant. They need to respect the musicians who they say they're honouring, but they don't. When they told me I was inducted they said, 'You have two tickets, one for your wife and one for yourself. Want another one? It's ten-thousand dollars. Sorry, that's the way it goes.' I said, 'What about my band? What about their wives?'."

Tensions were escalating rapidly, and when a Rock and Roll Hall of Fame publicist intervened to try to bring the proceedings to a close, it only added fuel to the fire. Miller reached his breaking point. "No we're not going to wrap things up. I'm going to wrap this up. You go sit over there and learn something," Miller said whilst holding two fingers up, according to the New York Times. "This is how close this whole show came to not happening. Because of the way the artists are being treated."

In the aftermath, there were lukewarm reactions and efforts to save face, with Hall members firing back in defence. According to The

New York Times, the Rock and Roll Hall of Fame issued a statement addressing the situation. "Rock and Roll can have many opinions. It's what makes it so great. We were honoured to induct Steve Miller and to congratulate him."

In a Rolling Stone interview, Hall of Fame President Joel Peresman strongly refuted Miller's accusations regarding the exclusion of women and the controversy surrounding the number of tickets. "At the end of the day, Steve Miller's unquestionable musical legacy and influence made him deserve to be inducted. That he feels this way, I feel badly for him. But again, we were thrilled and happy that he was inducted."

Unlike most rock and roll conflicts, Miller's outburst at the Rock and Roll Hall of Fame ceremony seemed poised to linger, largely due to Miller's apparent determination to keep the controversy alive. In a Time Magazine report, he would blast the people in the industry as "fucking gangsters and crooks", calling the Hall of Fame inductees "dicks and assholes".

In conversation with Rolling Stone, even Black Keys member Dan Auerbach had some harsh words to say. "We got a really uncomfortable feeling when we first met Steve. He had no idea who we were. No idea. The first thing he told us was, 'I can't wait to get out of here.' He knew that we signed up to do this speech for him and he made no effort to find out who we were."

As the verbal exchange persisted, it became evident to onlookers of this showdown that Miller, as portrayed in Rolling Stone, was relishing the conflict, seemingly content to intensify the dispute while championing those he felt deserved recognition. "All the industry people who had been sitting in the front row, like that guy who was there from my record label, I wanted to pull him by his necktie and kick him in his nuts. I came out to the ceremony for my fans, for the people who take it all seriously. Everybody else needs to stop all the bullshit. They need to put their books out there in the public."

"They need to stop lying."

Miller's criticism of the Hall of Fame would endure, spanning from 2016 to 2022. In interviews during this period, the controversy was consistently revisited, with Miller unapologetically expressing his disapproval. However, he also noted a slight softening of his stance, as he offered to Vulture.com.

"I pretty much have put it all behind me. I got so many calls from strangers and letters from people I didn't know wanting to talk about it. One person had a foot-high pile of documentation about the whole Hall of Fame thing, and I looked at it. I think the Hall of Fame is getting a bit better. It's very different every year since they first put the ceremony together."

Even this far down the line, Miller, as stated in Vulture.com, continued to hold the Hall of Fame accountable, refusing to relent in his criticism. "The year I was inducted, I think they were just making a television show and didn't care about us at all. It was really not a pleasant experience. It meant so much more to the world than to the people running it. I was so upset with the stuff I went through with them. We weren't even introduced to the other inductees. They never got us together. The whole thing was 'get your ass up there and then get off the stage because we're making a television show here'. For me, the whole experience was rude and cold."

Finally, Miller was willing to concede a couple of points. He admitted that in the cutting and editing of the show and, in general, they had matured a bit. "But I think they could do much better than just coming across as the snooty rock and roll place where their favourite people get eulogised. I never heard from them after that night. From their point of view, it was like 'next'. But I wouldn't have been interested in any case. I've pretty much moved on."

"I have other things to do."

Abracadabra

Slipping Into The Future

As Steve Miller hit the milestone of eighty years old in 2023, it seemed like the perfect setup for a blues tune. But far from slowing down, he was back on the road at the drop of a hat. Initially not planning to open for The Eagles' farewell tour in 2023/2024, fate intervened when a member of Steely Dan fell ill. Being the unrepentant road warrior he is, Miller jumped at the opportunity to join The Eagles on tour. This invitation couldn't have come at a better time psychologically for Miller. Turning eighty had brought him a sense of peace.

Speculation swirled around the musician, with talk of upcoming album anniversaries and discussions of re-releases and box sets. Yet, there were no concrete plans for new songs, and thankfully, no distractions or pressures from record companies to produce a hit. As he had often said over the years, it felt like an extended summer vacation at a laid-back summer camp.

"I'm looking forward to doing all these shows," he enthused in SteveMillerBand.com. "It's going to be a mighty time and a great summer."

Miller's perspective on being a card-carrying member of the classic rock generation had come full circle. Surviving long enough and achieving both commercial and creative success justified playing the hits alongside good friends like Peter Frampton and Neal Schon. Emotionally, it was the best gig an eighty-year-old could have.

This mindset played a significant role in Miller accepting an invitation to join Def Leppard, Journey, and, on select shows, Heart and Cheap Trick, for a three-month arena rock extravaganza extending well into 2024. Miller appeared genuinely humble about being part of such a superstar lineup, as he expressed in SteveMillerBand.com and PollstarNews.com.

"Hi everybody. I'm looking forward to doing these shows with Neal and Journey and the guys in Def Leppard. It's great to be surrounded by great talent and brilliant people that challenge me."

In 2024, Miller carved out time for more subtle and personal music, delving deeply into the blues and jazz roots that had long inspired him. Despite their smaller scale, the half-a-dozen intimate shows at The Jazz At Lincoln Centre allowed Miller to showcase himself in a more refined light. As detailed in The Wall Street Journal, he assumed the role of a teacher once again, offering nuanced and progressive interpretations of the musicians and influences that had shaped him.

Only two of Miller's greatest hits were featured in these shows, presented in subtle, fresh, and grounded renditions. Adding to the uniqueness of these sets were a handful of duets with emerging musicians, whom Miller confidently touted as the future of jazz and blues.

Despite the ripe opportunities for expansion in the past two years, Miller's focus eventually circled back to a fresh take on the song that propelled him to the top: 'The Joker'. In an interview with American Songwriter, he discussed his latest project, J50: The Evolution Of The Joker. This release, featuring ten tracks from the original 1973 album, and twenty-seven previously unreleased songs, would serve as an immersive educational experience for anyone aspiring to follow in Miller's footsteps.

"It's a look back at the magic moment when 'The Joker' came into being. The most important rule that every kid out there who wants to make a record should remember, is that when you go into the studio, be ready to do the whole performance the first time you do it. The whole thing is to capture that first performance. 'The Joker' was all first takes. And first takes are always better than perfect takes."

The End: It's That Simple

Steve Miller's journey has been anything but simple. From his life and times to his talent and attitude, he's remained a defiant figure, shaping his present and undoubtedly his future. With Miller, it's always been about living by his rules, ones he cherishes and upholds time and time again.

"It won't be long now," he emphasised in "In The Studio". "Just another few weeks and we'll be back on the road and I'll be excited and I'll be walking from the bus to the stage to play my music. And that's about as successful a life as I can have."

Appendix

They're In The Band

A lot of band members have spent time in The Steve Miller Band and keeping up with them all has been a herculean challenge. As of 3rd May 2024, the following members, their instruments and their time in the band is current. But be forewarned, the current lineup is subject to change at a moment's notice.

Current Members

Steve Miller
vocals/guitar/harmonica/keyboards
1966-Present

Kenny Lee Lewis
bass/backing vocals
1983-87/198-87/1994-present

Joseph Wooden
keyboards/backing vocals
1993-Present

Jacob Petersen
guitar/backing vocals
2011-Present

Ron Wisko
drums
2021-Present

Former members

Lonnie Turner
bass/backing vocals
1966-70/1973-78

Boz Scaggs
guitar/lead and backing vocals
1967-68

Jim Peterman
keyboard and backing vocals
1966-68

Tim Davis
drums/backing vocals
1966-70

James 'Curley' Cooke
guitar
1967

Ben Sidran
keyboard
1968-70/1972/1987-91

Nicky Hopkins
keyboards
1969-70

Bobby Winkelman
bass/backing vocals
1969-70

Ross Valory
bass/backing vocals
1970-71

Roger Allen Clark
drums
1972

Jack King
drums
1970-73

Dick Thompson
keyboards
1972-74

Gary Mallibar
drums/keyboards/backing vocals
1976-87

Gerald Johnson
bass/backing vocals
1972-73/1981-83

John King
drums
1973-74

Les Dudek
guitar
1975

Doug Clifford
drums
1975

Greg Douglass
slide guitar/backing vocals
1976-78

David Denny
guitar/backing vocals
1976-78

Byron Allen
keyboard
1976-87/1990

John Massaro
guitar/backing vocals
1982-83

Norton Buffalo
harmonica/guitar/backing vocals
1976-78/1987/1989-2009

Bill Peterson
bass/backing vocals
1987-2011

Bob Mallach
saxophone
1987-1996

Paul Peterson
guitar
1988/1991-92

Ricky Peterson
keyboards
1988-1991

Keith Allen
guitar/backing vocals
1989-1990

Sonny Charles
backing vocals
2008-2011

Gordy Knudtson
drums
1987-2021

Discography

While some of Steve Miller's albums didn't make it onto the charts and some singles weren't tied to albums, and some collections were only released in certain countries, most of his songs found their way to the public one way or another. For those of you dedicated to collecting everything from Steve Miller, here are the titles and release dates of his studio albums, singles, and live albums. Happy hunting to all the Steve Miller completists out there!

Studio Albums

Children Of The Future (June 1968)
Sailor (October 1968)
Brave New World (June 1969)
Your Saving Grace (November 1969
Number 5 (July 1970)
Rock Love (September 1971)
Recall The Beginning: The Journey From Eden (March 1972)
The Joker (October 1973)
Fly Like An Eagle (May 1976)
Book Of Dreams (May 1977)
Circle Of Love (October 1981)
Abracadabra (June 1982)
Italian X Rays (November 1984)
Living In The 20th Century (November 1986)
Born 2 B Blue (1988)
Wide River (June 1993)
Bingo! (June 2010)
Let Your Hair Down (April 2011)

Live Albums

Steve Miller Band Live (April 1983)
King Biscuit Flower Hour Presents The Steve Miller Band (July 2002)
Extended Versions (April 2003)
Steve Miller Band Live From Chicago (May 2008)
The Joker Live (May 2014)
Live At The Carousel Ballroom San Francisco April 1968 (September 2014)

Compilation Albums

Anthology (November 1972)
Greatest Hits 1974-1978 (November 1978)
Greatest Hits 1976-86: A Decade Of American Music (June 1987)
The Best Of 1968-1990: Living In The USA (1990)
Steve Miller Band (July 26, 1994)
Young Hearts: Complete Greatest Hits (September 16, 2003)
Ultimate Hits (September 15, 2017)
Welcome To The Vault (October 11, 2019)

Sources

100 Plus Songs.com
222. San Diego Reader
40 Year Itch.com
A Life In The Music book excerpt
A Load Of This.com
American Songwriter Magazine
Anti Music.net
Beautifulbox.com
Ben Sidran.com
Best Classic Bands.com
Betty Lou Music Acasemy.com
Billboard
Blogspot.com
Blues Highway.com
Blues Power Blog
Blues Power Blog
Brainy Quotes.com
Bruno Cerrito Early Years Website
Canton Rep. .com
CBS Morning News
CBS Sunday Morning News
Classic Rock.com
Concert Archives.com
Country Line Magazine
Digger Docs.com
Don's Tunes.com
Eight Miles High:
    Folk Rock From Haight Ashbury To Woodstock
Elsewhere.co.nz
Entertainment Weekly
For Bass Players Only
George Thorogood.com
Get Ready To Rock.com
Goldmine.com
Guitar Player.com
Guitar World.com
How Good It Is.com
Howard Stern satellite interview
Howard Stern Show
In The Studio.com
IORR.org
Isthmus.com
Joenickp.blogspot
Joker Live Press Release

Kensington
Let's Sing It.com
Louder Magazine
Loudersound.com
Milwaukee Journal Sentinel
Mix Online.com
New York Times
Offbeat Magazine
On Wisconsin Magazine
Oregonlive.com
Parade
Paul McCartney: So Many Years From Now
Peel Fandom.com
People
Pinterest.com
Pollstar.com
Pop Culture Classics.com
Power Pop.com
PRS Music.com
Record Collector
Red Bull Music Academy.com
Rock Prosgraphy 101.com
Rolling Stone
San Diego Reader
Sky Cloud Guru
Society Of Rock.com
Songfacts.com
Sound Man: A Life In Music
Steve Miller Band.com
Super 70's.com
Sweetwater Podcast.com
Syrius XM
Tampa Bay News Weekly
Texas Monthly Magazine
That Ericalper.com
The Aspen Times
The Austin Chronicle
The Big Interview
The Big Interview
The Coda Collection.com
The Dallas Morning News
The Dallas Observer
The Flaming Pie Archives Collector's Book
The Living Church

The Observer
The Oklahoman
The Paul McCartney Projects.com
The Record Producers
The Strange Brew.com
The Tennessean
The Washington Post
The Word
This Is Vinyl Tap.com
Tick Tick.com
Time
Tom Write Turns.com
U Discover Music.com
Ultimate Classic Rock
USA Today
USC News.com
Valparaisio University.com
Vintage Guitar.com
Vulture.com
Wall Street Journal
Weebly.com
Wickedlocal.com
Word Press.com

ABOUT THE AUTHOR

Marc Shapiro is the New York Times bestselling author of *J.K. Rowling: The Wizard behind Harry Potter*, *Justin Bieber: The Fever!* and many other bestselling celebrity biographies. He has been a freelance entertainment journalist for more than twenty-five years, covering film, television and music for a number of national and international newspapers and magazines.

authormarcshapiro@yahoo.com